new knits

erika knight

photography by Graham Atkins Hughes

new knits

20 knitting projects with a contemporary twist

quadrille

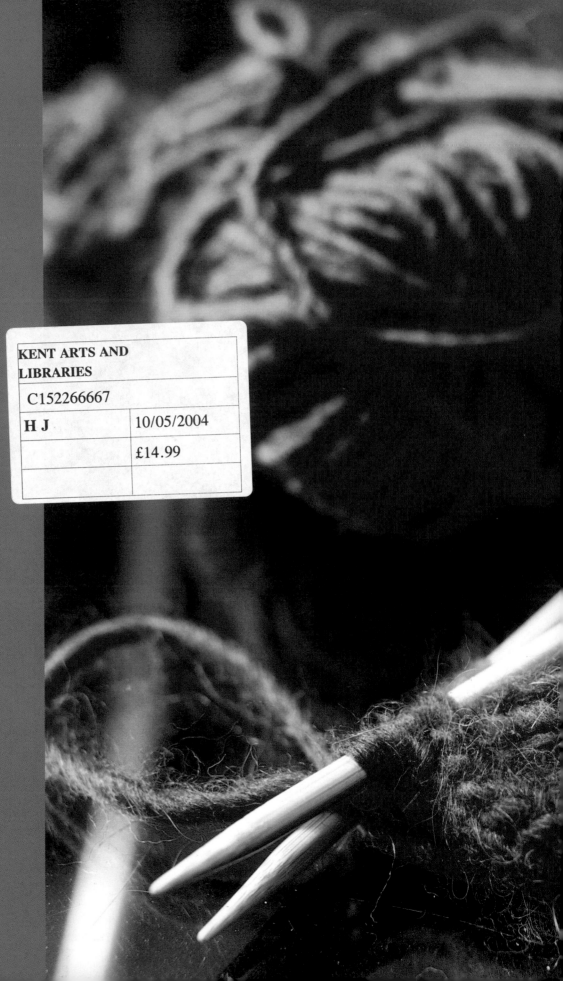

This book is dedicated to all the anonymous
people who have ever knitted, stitched and
created, going beyond function and
practicality for the passion of their craft.
They are, as always, my inspiration.

Editorial Director Jane O'Shea
Creative Director Helen Lewis
Project Editor Lisa Pendreigh
Pattern Checkers Marilyn Wilson and Eva Yates
Senior Designer Jim Smith
Illustrator Anthony Duke
Production Director Vincent Smith
Production Controller Jane Rogers

First published in 2004 by
Quadrille Publishing Limited
Alhambra House
27–31 Charing Cross Road
London WC2H 0LS

Text and project designs © Erika Knight 2004
Photography, illustrations, design and layout
© Quadrille Publishing Limited 2004

British Library Cataloguing-in-Publication Data
A catalogue record for this book is available from
the British Library.

ISBN 1-84400-084-2

Printed in Hong Kong

contents

techniques and textures

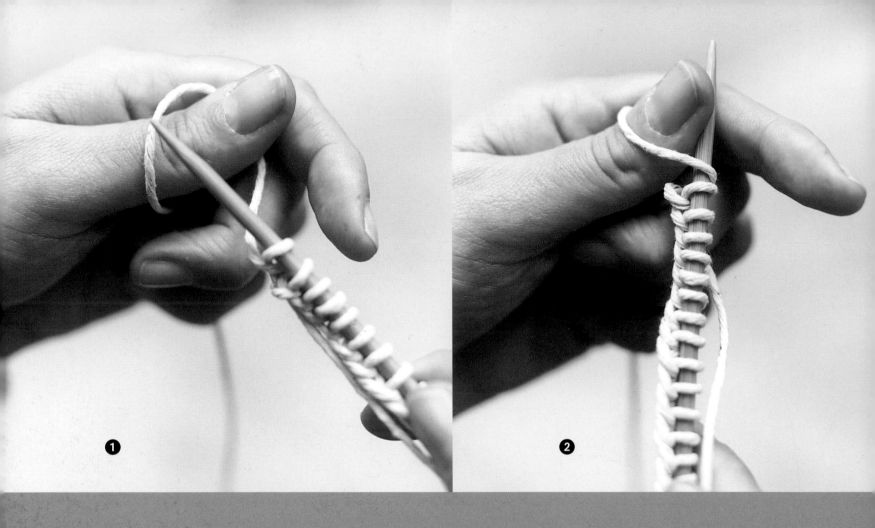

1

2

cast on

This is the very first thing you need to do in order to start knitting. Use this simple method of making the first stitches on a knitting needle using just a length of yarn and your thumb.

1 Leave a length of yarn that is long enough to create the number of stitches you are casting on (approximately 2.5cm for each stitch in DK-weight yarn, plus 5cm for insurance). Make a slip loop with the yarn and place it on a knitting needle. Hold the knitting needle with the loop of yarn in your right hand with the yarn from the ball. Take the loose end of the yarn in your left hand and form a loop around your left thumb.

3

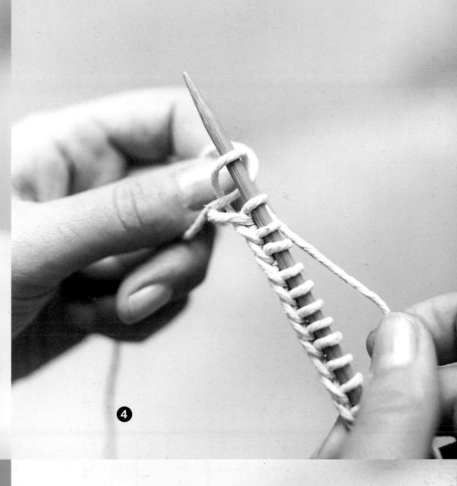

4

2 Insert the point of the knitting needle into the loop.

3 With your right hand, wrap the yarn from the ball over the point of the needle.

4 Pull the needle under and through the loop on your thumb.

5 Slip the loop off your thumb and gently tighten the stitch by pulling both strands. Repeat these steps until you have the required number of stitches.

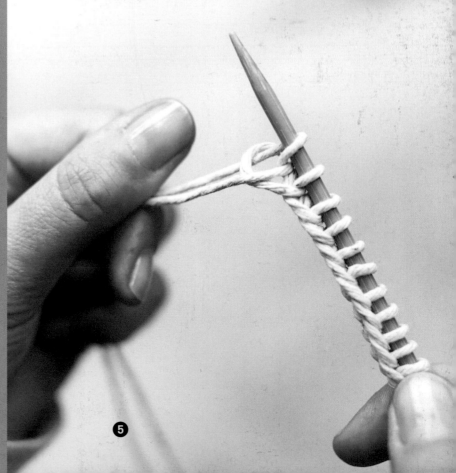

5

cast off

This is usually the very last thing you need to do in order to finish knitting. It is the process that fixes a piece of knitting so that it does not unravel once taken off the needles.

① At the beginning of your final row, knit the first two stitches as usual.

② Insert the point of the left-hand needle into the centre of the first knitted stitch.

③ Lift the first knitted stitch from the right-hand needle over the second knitted stitch on the right-hand needle.

④ Now remove the left-hand needle so only one knitted stitch remains on the right-hand needle. Knit the next stitch on the left-hand needle, so there are two knitted

stitches on the right-hand needle again. Repeat these steps, making sure there are never more than two knitted stitches on the right-hand needle.

⑤ Work until one knitted stitch remains on the right-hand needle. Cut the working yarn. Pass the end of the yarn through the last loop. Remove the needle and pull on the end of the yarn to tighten.

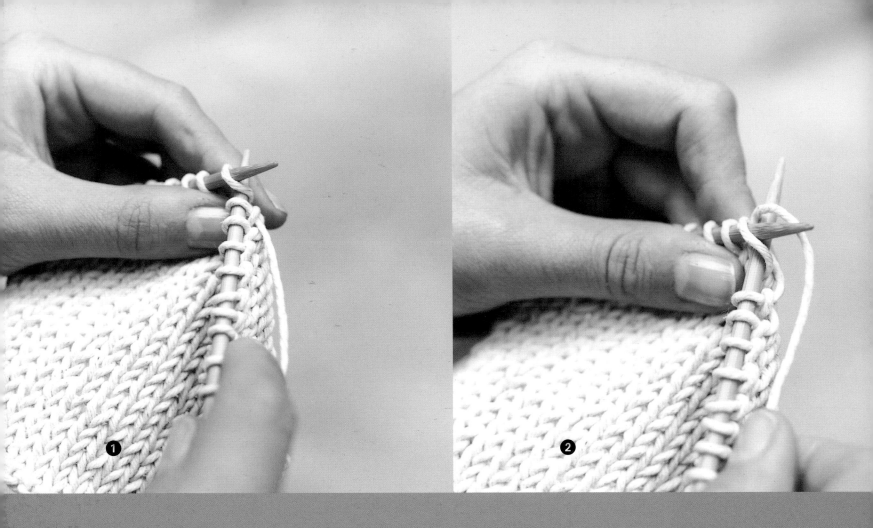

knit one

After casting on the appropriate number of stitches, as shown on page 8, you can begin to knit your first row. Each stitch is made by the simple four-step process shown here. Each row is completed by repeating this process until all the stitches on the left-hand needle have been transferred to the right-hand needle. Once you have completed each row, transfer the needle holding the worked stitches to your left hand and begin again. Another row of knit stitches will create a fabric known as garter stitch (see page 22).

❶ In – hold the needle with the cast-on stitches in your left hand, then holding the other needle in your right hand, insert the point of the right-hand needle into the first stitch

on the left-hand needle. Pass the needle under the loop facing you and up into the centre of the stitch so the needles form an X shape, with the left-hand needle in front of the right-hand needle.

❷ Over – holding the working yarn in your right hand, and at the back of the work, wrap the yarn over the point of the right-hand needle to make a loop.

❸ Under – slide the right-hand needle toward you, passing the point down and out of the centre of the stitch on the left-hand needle to pull the loop under and through the first stitch on the left-hand needle.

❹ Off – slide the original stitch off the point of the left-hand needle, leaving the new stitch on the right-hand needle. You have now knitted one stitch to the right-hand needle.

❶

❷

purl one

This stitch is worked in much the same way as the knit stitch, simply in reverse. When working the knit stitch, the yarn is held at the back of the work, but with the purl stitch, the yarn is held at the front of the work. Again, the purl stitch is made by the simple four-step process shown here. Repeat the process until the row is complete, and all the stitches have been transferred to the right-hand needle. Transfer this needle to your left hand before beginning the next row. Combining the knit stitch and the purl stitch provides the basis of all knitted fabrics, including the perennially popular stocking stitch, which is made by working one row knit, one row purl throughout (see page 22). The simple knit stitch and purl stitch is all there is to know!

1 Hold the needle with the cast-on stitches in your left hand. Holding the other needle in your right hand, and with the working yarn at the front of the work, insert the point of the right-hand needle into the front of the first stitch on the left-hand needle. Pass the needle from left to right through the centre of the first stitch.

2 Holding the working yarn in your right hand, and at the front of the work, wrap the yarn over the point of the right-hand needle to make a loop.

3 Slide the right-hand needle back and out of the first stitch on the left-hand needle to pull the loop under and through the first stitch on the left-hand needle.

4 Slide the original stitch off the point of the left-hand needle, leaving the new stitch on the right-hand needle. You have now purled one stitch to the right-hand needle.

make one

Adding stitches or taking away stitches – increasing or decreasing – shapes your knitting. There are several ways to increase, but the simplest method is to knit into the same stitch twice to make an additional stitch.

❶ Knit into the first stitch on the left-hand needle as usual and pull a loop through, but do not slip the original stitch off of the left-hand needle just yet.

❷ Instead, place the loop on the right-hand needle back onto the left-hand needle, effectively adding a new stitch to your knitting.

❸ Knit all the stitches in the usual way, including the new stitch just added.

③

If the increase is worked on a purl stitch, purl through the first stitch as usual, wrapping the yarn over the needle and pulling a new loop through, but leave the original stitch it on the left-hand needle. Insert the right-hand needle into the back of the same stitch on your left-hand needle and purl it again. Now slip the original stitch off the left-hand needle, leaving two stitches instead of the usual one on the right-hand needle.

take one

The simplest method of taking away stitches, or decreasing, is to knit two stitches together. Knitting the stitches together through the back of the loops (as shown here) forms a left-slanting increase, and knitting through the front of the a right-slanting one.

❶ Instead of inserting the right-hand needle into one stitch on the left-hand needle, insert it into the first two stitches at the same time.

❷ Holding the working yarn in your right hand, and at the back of the work, wrap the yarn over the point of the right-hand needle to make a loop.

❸ Slide the right-hand needle toward you, passing the point down and out of the centre

of the two stitches on the left-hand needle to pull the loop through the stitches on the left-hand needle.

4 Slide the original stitches off the point of the left-hand needle in the usual way, making sure that you drop both stitches from the left-hand needle. There is one stitch on the right-hand needle instead of two.

Decreases can also be worked on the purl row. Insert the point of the right-hand needle into the first two stitches on the left-hand needle at the same time and purl in the usual way, making sure that you drop both stitches from the left-hand needle. There is one stitch purled to the right-hand needle.

yarn textures

Let texture be your inspiration to design and make individual yarns to meet your personal requirements. It is not always easy to locate the specific yarns depicted in pattern books, either your nearest craft store is not that accessible or they do not have the yarns you want, the right colours or textures. So, what better than to create your own yarns from readily available sources?

You can use any continuous length of yarn to knit with, so it is just a matter of looking at an unconventional material in a different way and asking yourself whether it will meet your needs. Leather, wire, fabric, string, linen, tape, ribbon, felt, denim and rags, as well as more conventional wools, cottons and tweeds, each is an inspiration for a textile project.

stitch textures

The simplest of stitches can create the most effective textures. My favourite stitch is moss stitch as it creates a very firm fabric, which is especially good for homewear projects, with a very discrete self-colour pattern. An interesting variation is to work it in one strand of black yarn together with a strand of white yarn (see page 25).

Classic stocking stitch is great for cotton projects in particular. Alternatively, use the reverse side for more texture but less bulk than garter stitch, which is also easy to do and wonderfully textural.

Traditional Aran techniques look hugely professional; I like to create oversized cables, ribs and bobbles and use raspberry stitch for an all-over pattern.

◄ patch

Mix knitting with fabric for a contemporary twist to this traditional craft. Keep the patches simple in black and white, ecru or tones of a single colour. Experiment with materials such as suiting and shirting fabrics. Work in blocks and strips, then embellish with stitches by hand or machine to create a truly personal piece.

ply

Create your own random-effect yarns. Take strands of different coloured or textured yarns, twist together and then wind into a ball. Experiment with contrasting shades or black and white for a great marl effect.

undo

Seek out alternative sources of yarns and other materials: recycle old sweaters from the back of your wardrobe or discarded knitwear from charity shops. Launder and reuse them to create new projects. Unravel any knitted fabrics to knit the yarn up again or cut out any interesting details, such as cables or button bands.

redo

Re–assemble the pieces of knit into something new, such as the Customised Cushions (see page 70–3). Mix patterns, colours and different stitch textures. Or you may wish to recycle the sleeves of a favourite jumper and just add a newly knitted back and front. Create something unique yet inexpensive!

embroider

Simple embroidery stitches can be extremely effective for further embellishing knitting. Embroidery can be used to contrast against the knitted fabric or to complement the yarn for a subtler result. Use basic running stitches in random lengths to create a simple pattern on otherwise plain throws and cushions. Give your designs a further dimension by embroidering with chain stitch or edging a piece of recycled knitting with basic blanket stitch, at once functional and attractive.

modern
brights

rose chintz cushion

Tradition with a twist! Roses are a perennially popular decorative motif for interiors. This oversize rose chintz cushion creates a little drama for a chair or couch. Knitted in really chunky yarn, this shaped cushion takes no time at all to make. The leaves are worked in a melange of greens and the shading on the petals can be embroidered after knitting. Backed in a contrasting fabric, this cushion couldn't be easier to create.

see full chart on page 120

making the rose chintz cushion

materials

Rowan *Big Wool*
   Colour A: 2 x 100g balls in light pink
   Colour B: 1 x 100g ball in dark pink
   Colour C: 1 x 100g ball in black
Rowan *Biggy Print*
   Colour D: 1 x 100g ball in green melange
1 pair of 9mm (no. 00) knitting needles
Blunt-ended needle
Approximately 160 pink sequins
Approximately 150 black sequins
Large sewing needle
Sewing thread
0.5m fabric, 90cm wide (such as corduroy)
Dressmaker's chalk
Circular cushion pad, 41cm in diameter
Touch-and-close tape for fastening

size

One size (45cm in diameter)

tension

10 stitches and 14 rows to 10cm square over stocking stitch on 9mm (no. 00) needles. Always work a tension swatch and change needles accordingly if necessary.

tips

If working the rose as you knit, use the intarsia method; do not strand the yarn across the back of the work as this will distort the image. Use separate lengths of contrasting yarn for the coloured areas and twist the yarns together on the wrong side when changing colours to avoid any holes.

knitting the rose

Work the rose in stocking stitch – one row knit, one row purl alternately – from the full chart given on page 120. Read the chart from right to left on right side (knit) rows and from left to right on wrong side (purl) rows. Each square on the chart represents a stitch and each row of squares represents a row of knitting. Cast on and cast off stitches as indicated on the chart to shape the rose. Use a separate ball of yarn for each new colour change, twisting the strands of yarn at the back of the work to avoid any holes. (You may wish to wind small balls for separate areas to avoid tangling balls.) You may find it simpler to knit with colours A and D only, then embroider the petals in colours B and C afterwards with Swiss darning or duplicate stitch. This is a simple method of applying colour to a finished piece of knitting. Using Swiss darning or duplicate stitch is often quicker, easier and neater than knitting the colours in, as it leaves you free to concentrate on the knitting at hand.

embroidering the petals

Once you have knitted the basic rose shape, if required, embroider the petal colours B and C with Swiss darning or duplicate stitch. The embroidered stitch is worked on top of the knitted stitch in a contrasting colour. Using a blunt-ended needle and the required colour in a yarn of similar weight, darn the yarn invisibly at the back. * Then bring the needle up through the centre of the stitch from the back of the work, insert the needle from the right to the left, behind the stitch immediately above. Insert the needle through the centre of the original stitch and out through the centre of the stitch to the left, repeat from *.

sewing on the fabric backing

Weave in any yarn ends and press flat with a steam iron. Sew on the sequins as shown in the photograph, following the dark pink and black petal shading. Place the knitted rose on the backing fabric, right sides together. With dressmaker's chalk, draw around the shape of the rose. Allowing for a 1.5cm seam all the way round, cut the shape out of the fabric. With right sides together, sew the knitted rose and the backing fabric together, leaving an opening at the lower edge large enough to insert the cushion pad. Turn the cover right side out and insert the cushion pad. Sew touch-and-close tape along the opening for easy removal when cleaning.

retro poodle bottle cover

Simply kitsch! This retro look – once the domain of the Women's Institute and church hall bazaar – is now de rigueur. Adorn your sixties rosewood sideboard with the ultimate hostess accessory: a bottle cover for those pre-dinner shots. Knitted in two parts, this cute poodle is made in cotton yarn using simple moss stitch. The pompoms really make this design, while the beads for the eyes and embroidery for the nose both add character. And the velvet and diamante collar? Well, that just finishes it all off. Simply slip the cover over a standard 750ml spirit or wine bottle, break open the Twiglets and pass around the olives.

making the retro poodle bottle cover

materials

Rowan *Handknit DK Cotton*
   Colour A: 2 x 50g balls in pink
   Colour B: scraps of yarn in black
1 pair of 4mm (no. 8) knitting needles
Large sewing needle
2 small black beads
20cm black velvet ribbon

size

One size (to fit a standard 750ml bottle)

tension

18 stitches and 32 rows to 10cm square
over moss stitch on 4mm (no. 8) needles.
Always work a tension swatch and change
needles accordingly if necessary.

knitting the body

With 4mm (no. 8) needles and colour A,
cast on 17 stitches very loosely.
Row 1: knit to end. **Row 2:** purl to end.
Row 3: * knit 1, increase into next
stitch, repeat from * to last stitch,
knit 1. *25 stitches.* **Row 4:** purl to end.
Row 5: * knit 2, increase into next
stitch, repeat from * to last stitch,
knit 1. *33 stitches.* **Row 6:** purl to end.
Row 7: * knit 3, increase into
next stitch, repeat from * to last stitch,
knit 1. *41 stitches.* **Row 8:** purl to end.
Change to moss stitch – * knit 1,
purl 1, repeat from * to last stitch,
knit 1 – and continue, without shaping,
until knitting measures 21.5cm or height
to the neck of your chosen bottle from
cast-on edge.
Cast off in moss stitch. Join side seams
using mattress stitch.

knitting the head

With 4mm (no. 8) needles and colour A, cast on 33 stitches. Work 10 rows in moss stitch as on body.

Next row: knit 1, purl 1, knit 1, * purl 3 together, knit 1, purl 1, knit 1, repeat from * to end. *23 stitches.* Continue in moss stitch until knitting measures 9.5cm.

Next row: knit 1, purl 1, knit 1, * purl 3 together, knit 1, purl 1, knit 1, repeat from * to last 2 stitches, purl 1, knit 1. *17 stitches.* Work 3 rows in moss stitch.

Next row: knit 1, * purl 3 together, knit 1, repeat from * to end. *9 stitches.* Break off yarn, thread through the remaining stitches and fasten securely. Weave in any yarn ends and join side seams using mattress stitch.

knitting the nose

With 4mm (no. 8) needles and colour A, cast on 5 stitches. Continue in moss stitch as on body until knitting measures 6.5cm. Cast off in moss stitch. Sew cast-on edge to cast-off edge. Join one side and stuff with matching yarn. Join other side. Embroider over one end in colour B for nose. Sew to head as shown.

knitting the ears

With 4mm (no. 8) needles and colour A, cast on 9 stitches. Continue in moss stitch as on body until knitting measures 9cm. Cast off in moss stitch. Slightly gather cast-on and cast-off edges to curve and sew to head as shown.

making the pompoms

You need three different sizes pompoms – one large for the top of the head, three medium for the tips of the ears and tail, and six small, including four for the paws and two for the face.

Large pompom: wind the yarn around four fingers 75 times.

Medium pompom: wind the yarn around three fingers 60 times.

Small pompom: wind the yarn around three fingers 50 times.

Once the yarn has been wound around the requisite number of fingers the required amount of times, remove the yarn from your fingers and tie the bundle tightly in the middle. Cut through the loops on each side. Trim to a smooth round shape. Attach to the body and head as shown.

finishing the poodle

Sew on beads for eyes as shown. Join length of ribbon into circle for collar.

recycled plastic shopper

What can you do with mountains of plastic carrier bags that we all seem to collect? Recycle them, of course. Simply gather the bags, cut into strips and knit. This is such an easy project once you are used to working with the different textures of plastic. The simple handle is made from leather thonging – looped through the plastic and knotted – to give some precious contrast to the disposable plastic. Use the bag for storage just about anywhere in the home or garden, even in the kitchen as a container for collecting other plastic bags. Experiment with different colours, regular or random stripes, or use just a single colour for a completely even, chic look.

making the recycled plastic shopper

materials
Assorted plastic carrier bags, cut into
   strips (see below)
1 pair of 6.5mm (no. 3) knitting needles
Large sewing needle
Multipurpose polyproplyene string
   (available from hardware or stationers)
3.2m leather thonging, cut into two equal
   lengths of 1.6m

size
One size (38cm high by 32cm wide by 18cm deep)

tension
14 stitches and 20 rows to 10cm square over garter stitch on 6.5mm (no. 3) needles.
Always work a tension swatch and change needles accordingly if necessary.

cutting the bags into strips
Cut off the top section of each plastic
carrier bag to remove the handles.
Starting at the open top edge and
cutting through one side of the bag at
a time, cut a 2cm-wide strip in a spiral
all the way down the bag – a little like
peeling an orange – to make one
continuous length.
If the strips are too wide, simply cut
them in half again. If the strips are
too narrow, simply knit with two
strips together.
Knot different colour lengths together
as desired. Wind the strips into balls.

knitting the back
With 6.5mm (no. 3) needles, cast on
44 stitches. Continue in garter stitch –
knit every row – until knitting measures
38cm. Cast off.

knitting the front
Work as given for back.

knitting the gusset
With 6.5mm (no. 3) needles, cast on
20 stitches. Continue in garter stitch as
on back until knitting measures 106.5cm.
Cast off.

making up the bag
Starting at one end of gussett, pin
or tack the gusset to the back around
three edges, easing and straightening
to ensure the corners are square.
Repeat with the front to form the other
side of the bag. Using a large sewing
needle and polypropylene string, stitch
all the way round the pinned or tacked
edges with tiny running stitches. (Do not
use backstitch as this will distort the
knitted plastic.)

making the handles
Across the back, mark the position of
the handles with a coloured thread –
approximately 10cm in from each side
of the bag and 3cm from the top edge.
Thread the leather thonging from the
inside through to the outside of the
knitted bag at one marked point and
then back through at the other marked
point. Thread the thonging through twice
more and knot on the inside of the bag.
Repeat for the front.

woven woollen rug

This knitted rug is the simplest of projects to make for the home, and an economical way of recycling remnants of yarn in the age-old tradition. It's great if you are new to knitting, too, as it really is so quick and easy to make, and a little more functional than most first knitting projects! This is a new take on tubular knitting, where the different knitted strips are simply woven together to make a stylish textile for the floor. Alternatively, make this rug in tones of one hue to enhance the textures and coordinate with a particular colour scheme in your house.

making the woven woollen rug

materials
Assorted yarns from your remnants bag
– you will need approximately 50g of yarn
for one strip measuring 80cm long by
8cm wide
1 pair of 6.5mm (no. 3) knitting needles,
  or size for your chosen yarns
Large sewing needle

size
The size of this rug is determined by the length of the knitted strips, which can be
varied as required. The rug shown here measures 80cm long by 60cm wide.

tension
12 stitches and 16 rows to 10cm square over stocking stitch on 6.5mm (no. 3) needles.
Always work a tension swatch and change needles accordingly if necessary.

making a knitted strip

Cast on an even number of stitches. (The rug shown here is made of strips of 20 stitches.)

Row 1: * knit 1, yarn forward, slip 1 purlwise, yarn back, repeat from * to end. (The last stitch of every row is a slipped purl stitch.)

Repeat this row until work measures 80cm or required length.

Cast off by taking 2 stitches together – knit 2 together, knit 2 together, then slip the first stitch over the second – to end of row.

Thread the yarn through the end loop. Make a selection of both long and short strips.

weaving the knitted strips

Once you have made the required number of long and short strips, simply lay them out in a grid with the longer strips running lengthwise and the shorter strips running widthwise.

Weave all the strips together, working them over and under each other alternately.

Where the lengthwise and widthwise strips cross, secure each strip in place with small stitches using sewing thread.

patchwork throw

This fun-to-knit, reversible throw is made from three knitted strips, each one consisting of four different blocks alternately worked in stocking stitch, reverse stocking stitch and moss stitch. Two or three strands of yarn are used together to achieve this chunky look, which knits up really quickly. Contrasting borders are worked in tubular strips. Use the yarns specified in the pattern, or for your own individual look, work with a mix of leftovers from your remnants or the sale bin at your local yarn shop.

see full chart on page 121

making the patchwork throw

materials
Use a mixture of yarns selected for texture and effect. Use one strand of yarn on its own, or two or three strands together to achieve the correct weight and tension (see page 25). The following yarns were used to make the throw shown here:
Sirdar *Supa Nova Chunky*
  Colour A: 3 x 100g balls in mid pink
  (use two strands together)
Rowan *Como*
  Colour B: 7 x 50g balls in soft white
  (use three strands together)
Rowan *Polar*
  Colour C: 4 x 50g balls in purple
  (use two strands together)

Jaeger *Cadiz Cotton*
  Colour D: 3 x 50g balls in bright pink (use three strands together)
Rowan *Biggy Print*
  Colour E: 5 x 100g balls in multi pink (use one strand)
Rowan *Como*
  Colour F: 7 x 50g balls in light pink (use three strands together)
Rowan *Cork*
  Colour G: 5 x 50g balls in black (use two strands together)
1 pair of 9mm (no. 00) knitting needles and 1 pair of 8mm (no. 0) knitting needles
Large sewing needle

size
One size (168cm long by 130cm wide)

tension
8 stitches and 10 rows to 10cm square over stocking stitch on 9mm (no. 00) needles.
Always work a tension swatch and change needles accordingly if necessary.

preparing the yarns

Ply two or three strands of your selected yarns together to make one chunky yarn. If the yarn is already chunky, you may only need to use a single strand.

knitting the first strip of squares

With 9mm (no. 00) needles and colour A, cast on 34 stitches. Work the throw from the chart given on page 121. Read the chart from right to left on right side rows and from left to right on wrong side rows. Each square on the chart represents a stitch and each row on the chart represents a row of knitting.
Row 1: work across 1st row of chart for first strip in colour A, working in moss stitch as indicated.
Row 2: work across 2nd row of chart for first strip in colour A, working in moss stitch as indicated.

Continue as set, working in the stitch and yarn indicated, until first strip is complete. (Do not worry about the colour changes showing; it is a deliberate feature of this project, intended to add contrast.) Cast off.

knitting the second and third strips

Work as for first strip, following chart for second or third strip as appropriate.

knitting the border strips

With 8mm (no. 0) needles and colour E, cast on 16 stitches.
Row 1: * knit 1, yarn forward, slip 1 purlwise, yarn back, repeat from * to end. (The last stitch of every row is a slipped purl stitch.)
Repeat this row until knitting measures 152cm or same length as knitted strips. Cast off by taking 2 stitches together –

knit 2 together, knit 2 together, then slip first stitch over second – to end of row. Thread yarn through end loop. Make another border strip in the same way to the same length using colour A. Make two further border strips using colour B and colour F but to the shorter length of 129.5cm or the same width as the three strips plus the first two borders.

finishing the throw

Weave in any yarn ends and press flat with a steam iron, taking care not to flatten the stitch texture. Join the strips of blocks together lengthwise by oversewing using a single strand of yarn in a contrast color. Sew the borders to the edges of the throw, attaching the longer pieces first. Butt up the shorter border pieces to the top and bottom of the throw and sew in place.

black
and
whites

op-art wall hangings

Knitting doesn't only have to be worn. Simple knitted pieces can
be stretched over a canvas or frame and hung on the wall. Here,
the op-art paintings of the sixties have been re-invented with simple
knitted patterns for interior decoration. The flower, stripe and block
designs are all in graphic black and white, which can be further
embellished with chain stitch embroidery. There are three different
sizes given here, but it is such a simple principle that you could make
hangings to any size or shape. Here they have been worked in cotton
for clarity, but they can be made in any yarn, and embroidered,
appliquéd or even felted for an extra dimension. You can either work
the design into the piece or knit a plain background and Swiss darn
or duplicate stitch the pattern on afterwards.

see full chart on page 122

making the op-art wall hangings

materials
Rowan *DK Cotton*

flower
- Colour A: 6 x 50g balls in ecru
- Colour B: 2 x 50g balls in black
- Colour C: scraps in orange

stripes
- Colour A: 2 x 50g balls in ecru
- Colour B: 1 x 50g ball in black

blocks
- Colour A: 2 x 50g balls in ecru
- Colour B: 1 x 50g ball in black

Ready-made canvas, frame or plywood cut to size (available from most good craft stores)

1 pair of 3.75mm (no. 5) needles

Large sewing needle

size
flower 46cm square
stripes 25cm square
blocks 15cm square

tension
20 stitches and 28 rows to 10cm square over stocking stitch on 3.75mm (no. 5) needles. Always work a tension swatch and change needles accordingly if necessary.

tips
Work the design using the intarsia method, do not strand the yarn across the back of the work as this will distort the image. Use separate lengths of contrasting yarn for the coloured areas and twist the yarns together on the wrong side when changing colours to avoid any holes.

knitting the flower design
With 3.75mm (no. 5) needles and colour A, cast on 90 stitches. Work 22 rows in stocking stitch – one row knit, one row purl alternately.

Cast on 15 stitches at the beginning of the next 2 rows and at the same time work the flower from the full chart given on page 122 starting on the 16th stitch of each row. Read the chart from right to left on right side (knit) rows and from left to right on wrong side (purl) rows. Each square on the chart represents a stitch and each row of squares represents a row of knitting.

You may find it simpler to knit with colour A only, then embroider the flower in colour B afterwards with Swiss darning or duplicate stitch.

Cast off 15 stitches at the beginning of the next 2 rows. *90 stitches.* Change to colour A and work 22 rows in stocking stitch. Cast off.

embroidering with chain stitch
Lay a length of yarn over the knitted design, allowing it to curl and twist, then tack or tape it into position and follow the line in chain stitch. Alternatively, crochet a long chain, lay over the design and stitch into position.

knitting the stripe design
With 3.75mm (no. 5) needles and colour A, cast on 50 stitches. Work 22 rows in stocking stitch as on flower design. Cast on 15 stitches at the beginning of the next 2 rows and at the same time work the stripes from the chart given on page 123 starting on the 16th stitch of each row. Cast off 15 stitches at the beginning of the next 2 rows. *50 stitches.*

Change to colour A and work 22 rows in stocking stitch. Cast off.

knitting the block design
With 3.75mm (no. 5) needles and colour A, cast on 30 stitches. Work 22 rows in stocking stitch as on flower design. Cast on 15 stitches at the beginning of the next 2 rows and at the same time work the blocks from the chart given on page 123 starting on the 16th stitch of each row. Cast off 15 stitches at the beginning of the next 2 rows. *30 stitches.* Change to colour A and work 22 rows in stocking stitch. Cast off.

making up the wall hangings
Weave in any yarn ends and press flat with a steam iron. Lay the knitted design over the ready-made canvas, stretch into position and staple securely at the back.

barcode dog coat

Good and loyal pals deserve a little knitted attention, too! So what better than this barcode dog coat to make for your more-than-fair-weather friend. Knitted in one piece, the coat can be embroidered with your telephone number; after all you would want him to be safely returned should he choose to stray. Patterned in random stripes in graphic black and white, the coat is worked in stocking stitch with a detailed rib rollneck for a little rakish style. It is easy to pull over a dog's head without ties or buttons, nips or yelps!

making the barcode dog coat

materials
Rowan *Wool Cotton*
    Colour A: 2 x 50g balls in black
    Colour B: 1 x 50g ball in ecru
1 pair of 3.75mm (no. 9) knitting needles
1 pair of 4mm (no. 8) knitting needles
2 stitch holders or safety pins
Large sewing needle

size
One size (approximately 38cm chest and 34cm length)

tension
22 stitches and 32 rows to 10cm square over stocking stitch on 4mm (no. 8) needles. Always work a tension swatch and change needles accordingly if necessary.

tips
The dog coat is knitted in one piece in stocking stitch, worked in random stripes of 1, 2 or 3 rows in colours A and B alternately. Break off and rejoin yarns as necessary. When casting off around the neck edge, use larger size knitting needles to keep the rib loose and flexible.

knitting the body
Using 3.75mm (no. 9) needles and colour A, cast on 49 stitches. Work 3 rows in single rib – * knit 1, purl 1, repeat from * to last stitch, knit 1. Change to 4mm (no. 8) needles and stocking stitch, work in random stripes of 1, 2 or 3 rows but place plain band as follows:
Row 1: with colour A, knit to end.
Row 2: with colour A, purl 11, change to colour B, purl to end.
Continue pattern as set but at the same time increase 1 stitch at each end of next and every alternate row to 75 stitches. Increase 1 stitch at each end of every 3rd row to 83 stitches. Mark last row with coloured thread. Continue without shaping until knitting measures 18.5cm ending with wrong side row.
Divide leg openings: knit 14, turn.
Next row: cast off 2 stitches, purl to end.

Work 23 rows on these 12 stitches. Break off yarn and place onto stitch holder. With right side facing, rejoin yarn. **Next row:** knit 55, turn. Work 24 rows on these 55 stitches. Break off yarn and place onto a stitch holder. With right side facing, rejoin yarn. **Next row:** cast off 2 stitches, knit to end. Work 24 rows on these 14 stitches.
Next row: purl 12, cast on 2 stitches, purl 55 from stitch holder, cast on 2 stitches, purl 12 from stitch holder. *83 stitches.*
Shape neck: knit 10, knit 2 tog, knit 2, knit 2 tog through back loop, knit 51, knit 2 tog, knit 2, knit 2 tog through back loop, knit to end. *79 stitches.* **Next row:** purl to end. **Next row:** knit 9, knit 2 tog, knit 2, knit 2 tog through back loop, knit 49, knit 2 tog, knit 2, knit 2 tog through back loop, knit to end. *75 stitches.* **Next row:** purl to

end. Continue decreasing as set until 63 stitches remain. **Next row:** purl 30, purl 2 tog, purl to end. **knit polo neck:** using colour B, work 10cm in single rib as on body. Cast off loosely in rib.

making up the dog coat
Weave in any yarn ends and press flat with a steam iron. Referring to chart, embroider telephone number onto plain band in duplicate stitch. Join seam from top of polo neck to coloured thread. With 3.75mm (no. 9) needles and colour B, pick up and knit 67 stitches around inner bottom edge. Work 3 rows in single rib as on body. Cast off loosely. With 3.75mm (no. 9) needles and colour B, pick up and knit 21 stitches along side of left leg. Work 5 rows in single rib. Cast off loosely. Repeat along both sides of each leg opening. Join edges of rib.

patched throw

Using scraps of fabric to create a patchwork is a traditional way to
recycle. Here, however, patchwork has the addition of pieces of knitting,
which have been recycled in their turn by plying ends together to create
new yarns (see page 25). The selection of fabric and yarn is very
important: the simple theme of black and white adds a modern
dimension to patchwork, and will look dynamic in most interiors. The
instructions given here are more for inspiration. Select fabrics of your
choice in patches of suitable shapes and size, then tailor your knitted
pieces to complement and add texture and interest.

making the patched throw

materials

Fabrics: Keep it simple by using a limited number of fabrics – no more than 5 or 6 different types – as either the patchwork pieces or the appliqué. The throw shown here uses a striped fabric, a firm cotton ticking, a white wool (also used for the backing), a dogtooth check and a woven.

Yarns: Likewise, limit the knitting yarns to 2 or 3 and using basic stitches – stocking stitch, garter stitch, moss stitch, rib or slip stitches. Also, use the yarns as decoration in the form of running stitches, knots and tufts. The throw shown here uses ecru wool cotton, wool tweed and black chenille yarns.

Trims: The throw shown here uses plaid ribbon, gingham ribbon and scraps of the various fabrics for the appliqué.

1 pair of 9mm (no. 00) knitting needles
Large sewing needle
Sewing thread
Iron-on cotton interfacing

size

The size of the throw is determined by the size and shape of the patchwork pieces, which can be varied as required. The throw shown here measures 120cm by 105cm.

tension

12 stitches and 20 rows to 10cm square over stocking stitch on 9mm (no. 00) needles. Always work a tension swatch and change needles accordingly if necessary.

planning the throw

Using graph paper, work out the desired dimensions of the throw, including the distribution of the fabric and knitted pieces so you can see how to separate plains, stripes and knits. Sample the decorative effects on your fabrics.

cutting the fabric pieces

Cut all fabric pieces with a 2.5cm seam allowance all the way round. Back each piece of fabric with iron-on cotton interfacing (this helps to hold the shape).

decorating the fabric pieces

Decorate each fabric piece separately using a combination of effects:
a) Use the selvedge of the fabrics, as they often give a 'fancy' effect.
b) Fringe woven fabrics to make wide lengths or narrow strips or squares and oblongs, then top stitch on.
c) Draw threads out of the fabrics, either main pieces or smaller decorative ones.
d) Knit small patches or strips and apply using zigzag stitch by hand or machine.
e) Tie bows of ribbons, cord, string or frayed fabrics through the main pieces.
f) Use knitting yarns to sew uneven running stitches through the patchwork pieces to link them together.

making the knitted pieces

Knit the appropriate size pieces (test your tension first) and remember to include some seam allowance. As with the fabric pieces, back each knitted piece with iron-on cotton interfacing.

putting the throw together

Referring to your plan for positioning, machine or hand sew pieces together.

backing the throw

Cut a piece of woollen fabric, such as an old blanket, to the size of the patchwork plus seam allowance. Place the patchwork right side up on top of the backing fabric and machine around the edge.

quilting the throw

Apply any running stitches through the patchwork and backing fabric. Top stitch all patchwork pieces by machine or hand over the seams. At this stage any extra decorative appliqués can be machined on along with any wool embroidery.

finishing the throw

Add a ribbon edge or strips of contrast fabric by sandwiching throw in between the ribbon and butting ribbon ends at each corner of the throw.

laddered sweater

A favourite sweater is often regarded as an 'old friend', but there comes a time when it is beyond repair and, quite frankly, has seen far better days. But what makes you hold on to it? Its comfort, warmth and smell of familiarity makes you feel secure. It may have been a gift from a friend or family member, which creates a certain sentimental attachment. Well, this laddered sweater strikes a similar cord: knitted in soft, comfortable wool and with a well-worn, loved feel, it looks great and retains a certain urban appeal. The exaggerated ladders incorporated into the body of the sweater make amazing patterns – you could add more to make a 'cobweb' sweater or devise your own. Ladders are not a new technique in knitting, however. They were a feature of knitting even in the Victorian era, used for great decorative and intricate effect. Here I have just taken it a just a little bit further to give this sweater a deconstructed look.

making the laddered sweater

materials

Rowan *Chunky Merino*
  Colour A: 19 x 50g balls in ecru
  Colour B: 1 x 50g ball in black
1 pair of 7mm (no. 2) knitting needles
Stitch holder or safety pin and large sewing needle

size

small/medium   chest: 115cm   length: 68cm
medium/large   chest: 122cm   length: 72cm

tension

13.5 stitches and 19 rows to 10cm square over stocking stitch
on 7mm (no. 2) needles. Always work a tension swatch and
change needles accordingly if necessary.

knitting the back

Using 7mm (no. 2) needles and colour A,
cast on 66 (76) stitches. Work 2 rows in
single rib – knit 1, purl 1 to end. Change
to stocking stitch – one row knit, one row
purl alternately – and increase 1 stitch at
each end of 19th row and every following
20th row to 74 (84) stitches. (Make all
increases and decreases three stitches
n from the edge of the work.). Continue
without shaping until knitting measures
42.5 (45)cm ending with wrong side row.
Shape armhole: cast off 4 (5) stitches
at beginning of next 2 rows. Decrease
1 stitch at each end of next and every
alternate row until 58 (66) stitches
remain. Continue without shaping until
knitting measures 64 (68.5)cm ending
with wrong side row.
Shape shoulders and neck: knit to last
5 (6) stitches, turn. **Next row**: slip first
stitch, purl to last 5 (6) stitches, turn.
Next row: slip first stitch, knit to last
10 (12) stitches, turn. **Next row**: slip
first stitch, purl 4 (5) stitches, turn.
Next row: cast off 15 (18) stitches.
Break off yarn. With wrong side facing,
rejoin yarn. Cast off 28 (30) stitches
loosely purlwise, purl next 4 (5) stitches,
turn. *5 (6) stitches.* **Next row**: slip first
stitch, knit to end. Cast off 15 (18)
stitches loosely purlwise.

knitting the front

Using 7mm (no. 2) needles and colour A,
cast on 66 (76) stitches. Work 2 rows in
single rib as on back. Change to stocking
stitch and increase 1 stitch at each end
of 19th row and every following 20th row
to 74 (84) stitches (not including 'made'
stitches), but at the same time make the
random irregular ladders as follows

ensuring only 'made' stitches are
dropped when working the ladders:
Row 3 (ladder 1): knit 19 (24), make 1 –
pick up the loop between stitches and
knit into the back of it.
Row 5 (ladder 2): knit 33 (38), make 1.
Row 7 (ladder 3): knit 52 (57), make 1.
Row 11: knit 20 (25), make 1.
Row 13: knit 35 (40), make 1.
Row 17 (ladder 4): knit 9 (14), make 1,
make 1.
Row 19: knit 23 (28), make 1.
Row 25 (ladder 5): knit 31 (36), make 1.
Row 29: drop first make 1 to right of
ladder 1.
Row 31 (ladder 6): knit 70 (75), make 1.
Row 41: drop make 1 to left of ladder 2.
Row 43: drop ladder 2, drop make 1 to
left of ladder 1.
Row 45: drop ladder 1, make 1 to left of
ladder 6.

Row 51: drop make 1 to right of ladder 4.
Row 55: drop ladder 6 (2 stitches).
Row 63: make 1 before ladder 5.
Row 69: drop ladder 3.
Row 71: drop ladder 4.
Row 83: drop ladder 5.
Continue as for back until armhole shaping is complete and work measures 59 (65)cm ending with wrong side row.
Shape neck: knit 19 (22), leave remaining stitches on stitch holder.
Next row: purl to end. Decrease 1 stitch on neck edge on next and every alternate row until 15 (18) stitches remain.
Shape shoulder: purl to last 5 (6) stitches, turn. **Next row:** slip first stitch, knit to end, turn. **Next row:** purl 5 (6) stitches, turn. **Next row:** slip first stitch, knit to end. Cast off 15 (18) stitches. With right side facing, rejoin yarn.
Next row: cast off 20 (22) stitches, knit

to end. **Next row:** purl to end. Complete to match first side, reversing all shaping.

knitting the sleeves (make 2)
Using 7mm (no. 2) needles and colour A, cast on 40 (43) stitches. Work in knit 5, purl 3 rib for 5cm as follows:
Row 1: Purl 0 (3), * knit 5, purl 3, repeat from * to end. **Row 2:** * knit 3, purl 5, repeat from * to last 3 stitches, knit 0 (3). Continue in rib and increase 1 stitch at each end of next and every following 8th row to 58 (61) stitches, working extra stitches in rib pattern. (Increase using make 1 method rather than knitting twice into one stitch.) Continue without shaping until knitting measures 43 (45.5)cm ending with wrong side row.
Shape top: cast off 4 (5) stitches at beginning of next 2 rows. Decrease 1 stitch each end of next and every

alternate row until 14 (13) stitches remain.
Next row: knit 3, purl 2 tog, work across rib as set to last 5 stitches, purl 2 tog, knit 3. Decrease 1 stitch each end of every row until 6 (7) stitches remain. Cast off.

knitting the collar
With 7mm (no. 2) needles and colour A, cast on 64 (74) stitches. Work 16 rows in single rib. Change to colour B and work 1 row in single rib. Cast off loosely.

finishing the sweater
Weave in any yarn ends and press flat with a steam iron. Sew shoulder seams. Set sleeves into armholes between shaping and sew with mattress stitch, easing the ribs as you sew. Sew sleeve and side seams. Sew collar with fine backstitch so that the seam will show on the outside. Run ladders down.

customised cushions

Un-doing sweaters and other items of knitwear and then using that yarn to 'redo' something else was once a common practice. Now we have no shortage of new products to buy or material to make things from. However, this practice of recycling can be incredibly creative and spark great, individual ideas. Source old pieces of knitwear from charity shops, jumble sales, thrift stalls or from the back of your wardrobe, then cut up and reorganise the pieces. Cushions especially, are among the easiest and cheapest items to make or assemble in this way. Create numerous combinations with stripes, stitches, colours patterns and textures and bring a little seasonal touch and personality to your interior.

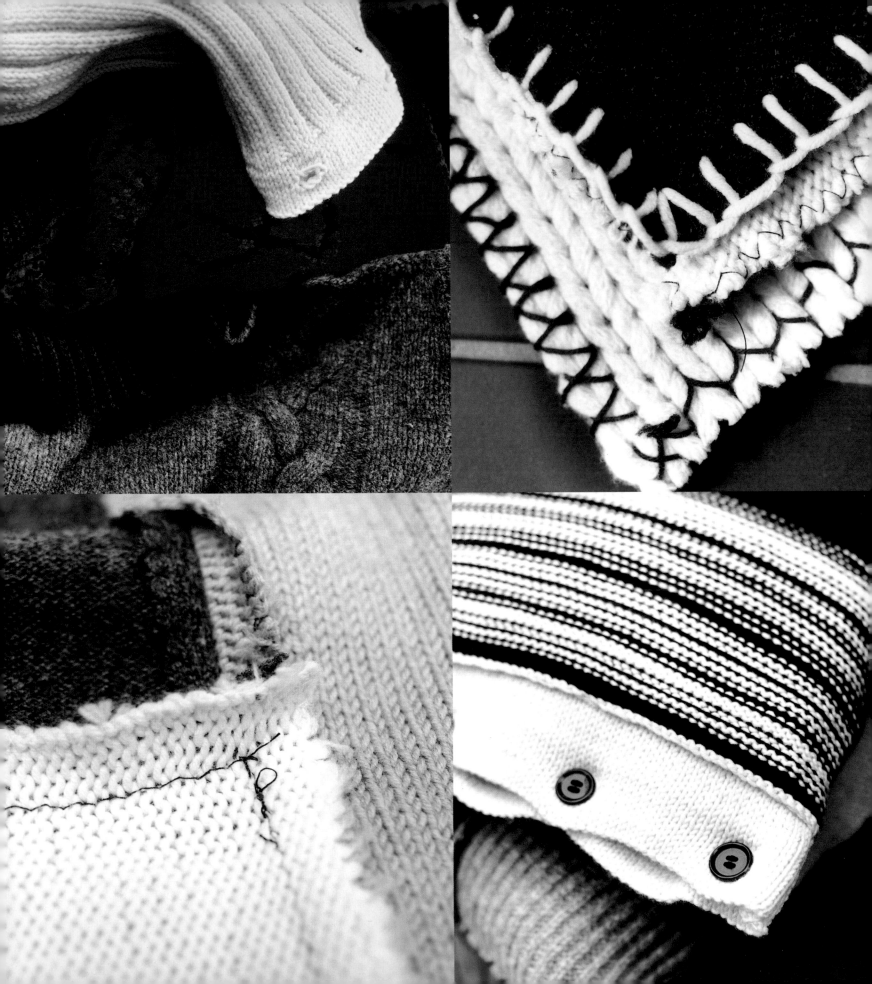

making the cushion front

Draw around the cushion pad to make a template for the cushion cover. Using the template as a guide, cut the knitted items into strips, squares, rectangles or other shapes to fit the shape of your cushion when put all together. There is no need to allow for a seam, as the cushion cover will fit better if slightly stretched over the cushion pad.

You may wish to incorporate necklines or fully fashion details in your design for added interest.

Once you have cut the cushion cover pieces either blanket stitch all around each piece by hand or alternatively overlock on the sewing machine.

Press all the pieces flat with a steam iron. Lay out the pieces into a design of your choice. Sew together by hand or machine to make the shape of the template.

making up the cushion

Cut a piece from a knitted item the same size as your cushion pad or template. Overlock all around the backing piece. With right sides together, sew the backing fabric to the cushion cover front together, leaving an opening large enough to insert the cushion pad at the lower edge. Turn cover right side out and insert cushion pad. Neaten up the cushion opening, attaching touch-and-close tape, press studs or tapes for easy removal when cleaning.

Alternatively, cut two pieces of knitted fabric for the cushion backing that make up the shape of the template when overlapped in the centre.

Overlock all around each backing piece. With right sides together, sew the two overlapping backing pieces to the cushion cover front together. Turn cover right side out and insert cushion pad.

Alternatively, incorporate the button band of a discarded cardigan into the design of your cushion front and back, making sure the buttons and buttonholes match up when making up the cushion.

You can further customise each cushion by adding embroidery or other embellishments, such as beads or sequins.

urban
neutrals

beaded napkin rings

Worked in wire adorned with iridescent beads knitted into the bands, these simple-yet-effective napkin rings make a unique addition to the urban table top. As they are very easy and quick to do, why not make one in a different colour for each member of the family or perhaps a matching set to coordinate for a party or special dinner. Contrast the wire and beads with matt linen napkins or sumptuous shantung silk for something precious.

making the beaded napkin rings

materials
Amounts given are for one napkin ring
7m coloured artists wire, 28 gauge
Approximately 120 iridescent beads in a
    complementary or contrasting colour
1 pair of 5.5mm (no. 5) knitting needles

size
One size (each napkin ring measures 15cm by 5cm)

tension
10 stitches and 12 rows to 10cm square over garter stitch on 5.5mm (no. 5) knitting
needles. Always work a tension swatch and change needles accordingly if necessary.

tips
It is important to thread the correct number of beads (or a few more than necessary)
onto the wire before starting to knit. Once the wire coil is started, it is difficult to add
more beads unless threaded from the other end of the wire or by breaking off and
rejoining the wire.

threading the beads
Check that the wire will pass through the
beads. Make a small loop at one end of
the wire and twist so that the beads will
stay on. Thread the beads onto the wire.

knitting the bands
Cast on 16 stitches, putting one bead on
every stitch as you cast on. As you bring
the wire around to make a stitch, slide
up a bead.
Knit to the end of the row, sliding up a
bead for each stitch knitted. Again, as
you bring the wire around to make a
stitch, slide up a bead first.
Knit 7 rows in this way.
Cast off, putting a bead on every stitch
as you cast off.
Leave a long end (approximately 10cm)
to use when making up the knitted band
into a ring.

making up the rings
Bend the knitted band into a ring and
thread the wire all along the seam to
fasten together.

satin boudoir slippers

Ribbon is a beautiful and readily available material for knitting. There is a huge variety currently on the market, from satins, velvets and organzas to ginghams and brocades. Ribbon has a gorgeous sheen and depth of colour, and creates a uniquely textured fabric with a character all of its own. These simple slippers are worked in double-sided satin ribbon to create a luxurious yet firm fabric. Make them as a gift or for yourself as pretty accessories for the bedroom. Lined with an insole covered in silk dupion and decoratively adorned with ribbon ties, they are both pretty and practical.

making the satin boudoir slippers

materials

Amounts given are for one pair of slippers

Approximately 95 (100: 110)m double-
  sided satin ribbon, 1cm wide

1 pair of 5.5mm (no. 5) knitting needles

Large sewing needle

Pair of insoles

Approximately 20cm silk dupion

Fabric glue

size

to fit average UK shoe size 3–4 (5–6: 7–8) – actual length 21 (23: 25)cm

tension

14 stitches and 19 rows to 10cm square over stocking stitch on 5.5mm (no. 5) needles. Always work a tension swatch and change needles accordingly if necessary.

knitting the sole and heel

With 5.5mm (no. 5) needles, cast on 6 (8: 10) stitches. Work 2 rows in stocking stitch – knit 1 row, purl 1 row. Increase 1 stitch at each end of next and every alternate row to 12 (14: 16) stitches. Continue in stocking stitch until knitting measures 21 (23: 25)cm ending with wrong side row. Decrease 1 stitch at each end of next and every alternate row until 6 (8: 10) stitches remain. **Next row (right side row):** purl to end. (This row makes the ridge where the heel is folded.) **Next row:** increase 1 stitch at each end of next and every alternate row to 12 (14: 16) stitches.
Next row: purl to end.
Cast on 8 (8: 8) stitches at the beginning of the next 2 rows. *28 (30: 32) stitches.* Work 2 rows in stocking stitch.
Next row: decrease 1 stitch at each end of next 4 rows. *20 (22: 24) stitches.* Cast off.

knitting the upper

With 5.5mm (no. 5) needles, cast on 6 (8: 10) stitches. Work 2 rows in stocking stitch as on sole. Increase 1 stitch at each end of next and every alternate row to 12 (14: 16) stitches.
Next row: purl to end. **Next row:** knit 3, make 1 by picking up loop between next stitch, knit to last 3 stitches, make 1, knit to end.
Continue increasing in this way on every knit row to 20 (22: 24) stitches. Continue in stocking stitch until knitting measures 12 (13: 14)cm. Cast off.

making up the slippers

Weave in any yarn ends and and press flat with a steam iron. With wrong sides facing, fold at the heel line and sew each side of the heel to the sole creating the seam on the outside. Pin the upper into position, overlapping the side points, and stitch, securing the overlap with an extra stitch. Attach ribbon to the sides for ties.

making the insoles

Cut insoles to the required shoe size. Trace around the insoles on the silk dupion, leaving a 1cm allowance, and cut out the fabric shapes.
Cover the top of the insoles with the cut fabric and glue in place on underside. Cut two additional insole shapes from the fabric but without the 1cm allowance. Glue in place on the underside of the insoles covering any raw fabric edges. Allow glue to dry thoroughly before inserting into finished slipper.

painted felt cushion

The top of this cushion cover is a square of textural knitting made from a homemade yarn: a piece of felt embellished with metallic fabric paint, then cut into one long strip and wound into a ball. The knitted square is then sewn up into a basic cushion cover with two extra pieces of plain felt fabric. Use this simple technique to create your own personalised yarns of different colours and textures. As felt has such a wonderful sueded quality, you may even be inspired to make your own felt and incorporate random colours as you go.

making the painted felt cushion

materials
Approximately 2m felt, 100cm wide
Fabric paint in complementary or
    contrasting colour and paintbrush
1 pair of 5.5mm (no. 5) knitting needles
Large sewing needle
Sewing thread
Cushion pad, 46cm square

size
One size (each cushion measures 46cm square)

tension
6 stitches and 8 rows to 10cm square over stocking stitch on 5.5mm (no. 5) needles.
Always work a tension swatch and change needles accordingly if necessary.

tips
You may find it easier to cut the felt into a few manageable-sized pieces before
painting. If you do this, do not worry about geeting a seamless join when adding in
a new length of yarn as the knitted surface will be highly textural.

making the cushion back
Cut two pieces of felt 46cm wide by
39.5cm long.
Overlap these two pieces so that they
make a square measuring 46cm by 46cm.
Pin into position.

painting and cutting the felt
Lay the remainder of the felt out flat.
Using a paintbrush, paint horizontal
stripes on to the felt approximately
2.5cm apart. Allow to dry.
Working from right to left, cut the felt
into a strip along the first painted stripe
almost to the left edge, but leaving
approximately 2cm uncut. Change
direction and cut from left to right along
the second painted stripe again leaving
approximately 2cm uncut at the right
edge. Cut the rest of the felt in this way
to make one continuous length of fabric.

knitting the cushion front
With 5.5mm (no. 5) knitting needles, cast
on 24 stitches.
Continue in stocking stitch – knit 1 row,
purl 1 row alternately – until work
measures 46cm.
Cast off.

making up the cushion
Pin the cushion backs to the reverse
side of the knitted cushion front. You
may prefer the reverse stocking stitch
side to the stocking stitch side, it's
your choice.
Stitch seams all the way round on the
right side, either by hand or by machine,
to leave a pronounced external seam.
Insert the cushion pad through the
flap opening.

moulded wire bowls

Wire has often been used for knitting, most spectacularly in the arena of costume design for the theatre. Surprisingly, wire is very easy to knit with and is available in the most stunning colours. Worked on two needles and in simple stocking stitch, knitted fabric takes on a wholly different character in wire. The very best part of this project is shaping the bowl once it is knitted – mould it, twist it, bend it, fold it, distort it, personalise it. Use the bowls to hold bonbons or jewellery, or make several in different sizes, shapes and colours and cluster them together. Experiment.

making the
moulded wire bowls

materials
1 (3) x 50g reel of coloured artistic wire,
  24 gauge (0.5mm
1 pair of 5.5mm (no. 5) knitting needles

size
small bowl measures 12cm high by 43cm
in circumference
large bowl measures 12cm high by 53cm
in cicumference

tension
14 stitches and 17 rows to 10cm square over
stocking stitch on 5.5mm (no. 5) needles.
Always work a tension swatch and change
needles accordingly if necessary.

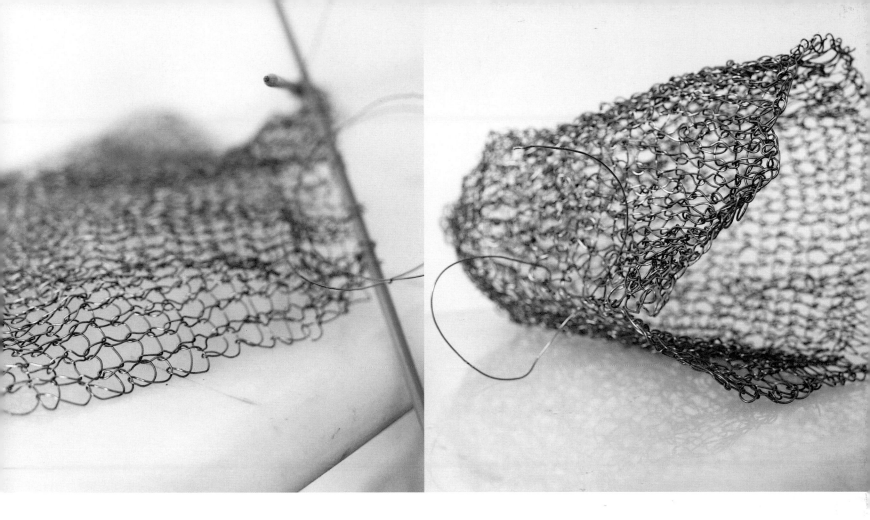

knitting the bowl

Cast on 61 (75) stitches.

Work 4 rows in stocking stitch – knit 1 row, purl 1 row alternately.

Next row: * knit 8, knit 2 together, repeat from * to last 1 (5) stitches, knit 1 (5).

55 (68) stitches.

Work 3 rows in stocking stitch.

Next row: * knit 7, knit 2 together, repeat from * to last 1 (5) stitches, knit 1 (5).

49 (61) stitches.

Work 3 rows in stocking stitch.

Next row: * knit 6, knit 2 together, repeat from * to last 1 (5) stitches, knit 1 (5).

43 (54) stitches.

Work 3 rows in stocking stitch.

Next row: * knit 5, knit 2 together, repeat from * to last 1 (5) stitches, knit 1 (5).

37 (47) stitches.

Next row: purl to end.

Next row: * knit 4, knit 2 together, repeat from * to last 1 (5) stitches, knit 1 (5).

31 (40) stitches.

Next row: knit to end. (This row makes the ridge that forms the base.)

Next row: * knit 3, knit 2 together, repeat from * to last 1 (0) stitch, knit 1 (0).

25 (32) stitches.

Next row: purl to end.

Next row: * knit 2, knit 2 together, repeat from * to last 1 (0) stitch, knit 1 (0).

19 (24) stitches.

Next row: purl to end.

Next row: * knit 1, knit 2 together, repeat from * to last 1 (0) stitch, knit 1 (0).

13 (16) stitches.

Next row: purl to end.

Next row: * purl 2 together, repeat from * to last 1 (0) stitch, purl 1 (0).

7 (8) stitches.

Do not cast off but leave a long end (approximately 15cm) to use when joining the knitting into a bowl.

making up the bowl

Bend the knitted bowl so the edges are together and thread the long end of the wire through the remaining stitches on the needle. Pull the stitches up tight. Thread the wire all along the edges to fasten together. Mould the bowl by gently pulling into shape.

flower-trimmed evening bag

Beautifully feminine and totally frivolous! This little bag is knitted on large needles with net fabric cut into strips. It is made from a long rectangular shape worked in simple garter stitch and then sewn together. The corners are folded in and stitched to make a gusset. It is lined in a sumptuous tonal satin, trimmed with sueded ribbon handles and decorated with wired ribbon and a flower corsage made of net and organza. It is easy to make but enormously effective. Alternatively, make the bag in black for added glamour or in vivid vibrant colours just for fun. The perfect girly accessory.

making the flower-trimmed evening bag

materials

Approximately 7m net fabric, 70cm wide,
   cut into strip (see below)
1 pair of 9mm (no. 00) knitting needles
Scraps of net and organza for flower
Approximately 200 iridescent sequins
   for flower
1.5m wired ribbon, 4cm wide, for trim
82cm sueded ribbon, 2.5cm wide,
   for handles
50cm satin, 70cm wide, for lining
Sewing needle
Sewing thread

size

One size (each bag measures approximately 32cm wide by 25cm deep)

tension

14 stitches and 21 rows to 10cm square over garter stitch on 9mm (no. 00) needles.
Always work a tension swatch and change needles accordingly if necessary.

tips

Net can be a little slippery and springy, and has a tendency to move around when
being cut. Don't worry if some strips end up wider or thinner than others.

cutting the net

Lay the net out flat. Working from right
to left, cut the net into a strip about
2.5cm wide almost to the left edge,
but leaving approximately 2cm uncut.
Change direction and cut the net into
a strip from left to right again leaving
approximately 2cm uncut at the right
edge. Cut the rest of the net in this way
to make one continuous length of fabric.

knitting the bag

With 9mm (no. 00) knitting needles, cast
on 41 stitches. Continue in garter stitch –
knit every row – until knitting measures
61cm. Cast off. Use the knitted outer as a
template to cut the satin lining to the same
size, plus an extra 2cm seam allowance.

making up the bag

Fold the knitting in half widthways.

Sew side seams by hand or machine. To
form the bag's base and gusset, take the
tips of the sewn corners and fold inwards
to form a box shape (like wrapping the
edges of a parcel). Catch the folded
corners to the base of the bag with a few
tacking stitches. Turn right side out.

attaching the handles

Stitch the ribbon handles to the inside
of the bag approximately 10cm apart and
10cm in from the side edge.

lining the bag

With right sides together, fold the cut
satin in half widthwise. As with the
knitted outer, sew side seams by hand
or machine then create the base and
gusset in the same way. Catch the
folded corners to the base of the lining
with a few tacking stitches. Place the

lining inside the knitted outer, with right
side visible. Fold the top 2cm of the lining
inside the bag to neaten. Hand stitch
lining to top edge of bag to secure.

making the flower

Cut 'rounded' bow shapes from the
scraps of net and organza for the petals.
Add sequins to the edges of each cut
petal. Layer the sequin-trimmed petals
one on top of the other, alternating the
net and organza, and mould into shape.
Stitch together at centre.

attaching the trim

Wrap the ribbon around the bag
approximately 5cm down from the top
and tie in a simple bow. Stitch into
position. Sew the flower into position
near the ribbon bow, as shown in
the photograph.

organic
naturals

aran armchair cover

A woolly sweater for your favourite armchair! Great to cuddle into on chilly afternoons, this loose chair cover is really much easier to knit than first impressions suggest. It is worked in chunky natural tweed wool to parody the classic fisherman's sweater, incorporating traditional Aran patterns that are oversized for increased impact. To keep it manageable, each panel is worked separately with very simple shaping. This cover fits a classic club chair, which is widely available, but with a little alteration can be adapted to cover a different shape.

making the aran armchair cover

materials

Rowan *Rowanspun Chunky*
  22 x 100g hanks in ecru
1 pair of 6.5mm (no. 3) knitting needles
Cable needle
Approximately 2m cotton tape, cut into
  25cm lengths
Large sewing needle
Sewing thread

size

One size (to fit a Tullsta tub chair from Ikea, approximately 80cm wide, 72cm deep, 78cm high and 43cm seat depth)

tension

13.5 stitches and 19 rows to 10cm square over stocking stitch on 6.5mm (no. 3) needles. Always work a tension swatch and change needles accordingly if necessary.

tips

When knitting the Aran pattern, it is possible to knit the bobbles separately, leave them on a long thread and sew into place when making up.

When shaping, mark the first increase or decrease with a coloured thread so you can see on which side they have been made.

You will need the following stitches to knit the Aran Armchair Cover:

reverse stocking stitch
Row 1 (right side): purl.
Row 2: knit.
Repeat the last 2 rows.

moss stitch
On an odd number of stitches:
Every row: * knit 1, purl 1, repeat from * to last stitch, knit 1.
On an even number of stitches:
Row 1: * knit 1, purl 1, repeat from * to end.
Row 2: * purl 1, knit 1, repeat from * to end.
Repeat the last 2 rows.

raspberry stitch
The following stitch is incorporated into the raspberry stitch pattern:
m2 (make 2 stitches): knit 1, purl 1, knit 1 all into next stitch.

Worked over 4 stitches:
Row 1 (right side): purl.
Row 2: knit 1, * m2, purl 3 together [bobble], repeat from * to last stitch, knit 1.
Row 3: purl.
Row 4: knit 1, * purl 3 together, m2, repeat from * to last stitch, knit 1.
Repeat the last 4 rows.

twisted stitch
The following stitch is incorporated into the twisted stitch pattern:
tw2 (twist 2 stitches): knit second stitch but leave on left-hand needle, then knit first stitch, slip both stitches off needle together.

Worked over 2 stitches:
Row 1 (right side): tw2.
Row 2: purl.
Repeat the last 2 rows.

diamond panel
The following stitches are incorporated into the diamond panel:
mb (make bobble): knit into back and front of same stitch twice, * turn, purl these 4 stitches, turn, knit these 4 stitches, repeat from * once, slip second, third and fourth stitches over first stitch.

c5f (cross 5 front): slip next 2 stitches onto a cable needle and hold at front of work, knit 2 stitches and purl 1 stitch from left-hand needle, knit 2 stitches from cable needle.

t3b (twist 3 back): slip next stitch onto a cable needle and hold at back of work, knit 2 stitches from left-hand needle, purl 1 stitch from cable needle.

t3f (twist 3 front): slip next 2 stitches onto a cable needle and hold at front of work, purl 1 stitch from left-hand needle, knit 2 stitches from cable needle.

Worked over 13 stitches on a background of reverse stocking stitch:

Row 1 (right side): purl 1, mb, purl 2, c5f, purl 2, mb, purl 1.
Row 2: knit 4, purl 2, knit 1, purl 2, knit 4.
Row 3: purl 3, t3b, knit 1, t3f, purl 3.
Row 4: knit 3, purl 2, knit 1, purl 1, knit 1, purl 2, knit 3.
Row 5: purl 2, t3b, knit 1, purl 1, knit 1, t3f, purl 2.
Row 6: knit 2, purl 2, [knit 1, purl 1] twice, knit 1, purl 2, knit 2.
Row 7: purl 1, t3b, [knit 1, purl 1] twice, knit 1, t3f, purl 1.
Row 8: knit 1, purl 2, * knit 1, purl 1, repeat from * twice, knit 1, purl 2, knit 1.
Row 9: t3b, * knit 1, purl 1, repeat from * twice, knit 1, t3f.
Row 10: purl 2, * knit 1, purl 1, repeat from * three times, knit 1, purl 2.
Row 11: t3f, * purl 1, knit 1, repeat from * twice, purl 1, t3b.
Row 12: as row 8.
Row 13: purl 1, t3f, [purl 1, knit 1] twice, purl 1, t3b, purl 1.
Row 14: as row 6.
Row 15: purl 2, t3f, purl 1, knit 1, purl 1, t3b, purl 2.
Row 16: as row 4.
Row 17: purl 3, t3f, purl 1, t3b, purl 3.
Row 18: as row 2.
Repeat these 18 rows.

fat cable

Worked over 22 stitches on a background of reverse stocking stitch:
c8b, c8f (cable 8 back, cable 8 front): slip next 4 stitches onto a cable needle and hold at back or front of work, knit 4 stitches from left-hand needle then 4 stitches from cable needle.

Row 1 (right side): purl 3, knit 16, purl 3.
Row 2: knit 3, purl 16, knit 3.
Row 3: purl 3, c8b, c8f, purl 3.
Row 4: knit 3, purl 16, knit 3.
Rows 5–12: repeat rows 1 and 2 four times.
Repeat these 12 rows.

making piece A (left outer side panel)

With 6.5mm (no. 50 needles), cast on 58 stitches and work in rib as follows:
Row 1 (right side): * knit 3, purl 2, repeat from * to last 3 stitches, knit 3.
Row 2: * purl 3, knit 2, repeat from * to last 3 stitches, purl 3.
Repeat these 2 rows until knitting measures 12.5cm ending with wrong side row.
Change to moss stitch and increase 1 stitch at beginning of every 12th row to 65 stitches. (Mark first increase with a coloured thread, as all increases must be on the same side.)
Continue in moss stitch without shaping until knitting measures 44cm ending with wrong side row.
Shape top: cast off 9 stitches at beginning of next and every alternate row until 11 stitches remain. Cast off.

making piece B (right outer side panel)

Work as given for A (left outer side panel) but reversing all shaping.

making piece C (right back panel)

With 6.5mm (no. 5) needles, cast on 53 stitches and work 12.5cm in rib as on A (left outer side panel) ending with a wrong side row.
The back panels have a 2-stitch garter

stitch border at centre back edge, which starts after the rib.
Next row: change to moss stitch, working 2 stitches of garter stitch border at end of row [centre back]. Continue as set until knitting measures 52cm ending with wrong side row.
Shape top: cast off 7 stitches at beginning of next and every alternate row until 11 stitches remain. Cast off.

making piece D (left back panel)

Work as given for C (right back panel) but reversing all shaping. Remember to work the garter stitch border at beginning of first row [centre back].

making piece E (left inner side panel)

With 6.5mm (no. 5) needles, cast on 62 stitches and work in raspberry stitch, increasing 1 stitch at beginning of every 5th row to 75 stitches. (Mark first increase with a coloured thread, as all increases must be on the same side. Also, when increasing in raspberry stitch, make a new bobble only when you have increased 4 stitches, not before, or you will have too many stitches on the needle.)
Continue without shaping until knitting measures 43cm ending with right side row.
Shape top: cast off 11 stitches on next and every alternate row until 9 stitches remain. Cast off.

making piece F (right inner side panel)

Work as given for E (left inner side panel) but reversing all shaping.

making piece G (centre back panel)

With 6.5mm (no. 5) needles, cast on 78 stitches and work the Aran pattern as follows:

Row 1 (right side): purl 7; work 64 stitch Aran pattern as follows – tw2, purl 2, 13 stitches from diamond panel, purl 2, tw2, 22 stitches from fat cable, tw2, purl 2, 13 stitches from diamond panel, purl 2, tw2; purl 7.

Row 2: knit 7, work row 2 of Aran pattern, knit 7.

Increase 1 stitch at each end of every 16th row until 86 stitches on needle, and then increase at each end of every 3rd row until 100 stitches on needle, and making bobbles (mb) at centre of extra stitches on every row 1 of diamond panel (see photograph). (All extra stitches are worked in reverse stocking stitch.)

Continue without shaping until knitting measures 48cm.

Shape top by decreasing 1 stitch at each end of next 15 rows. *70 stitches.*

Cast off 2 stitches at beginning of next 9 rows. *52 stitches.* Cast off.

making piece H (front panel, including arm fronts)

Cast on 118 stitches and work 12.5cm in rib as on A (left outer side panel).

Referring to the photograph, now work in pattern as follows:

Next row: 22 stitches from fat cable, purl 5, work 64 stitches from Aran pattern as on centre back panel (piece G), purl 5, 22 stitches from fat cable.

This sets the pattern. Continue in pattern until knitting measures 18cm ending with wrong side row.

Work across first 22 stitches (fat cable) and place onto stitch holder or spare yarn, work across next 74 stitches, place last 22 stitches onto stitch holder or spare yarn. Continue on 74 stitches in pattern until knitting measures 37cm from start.

Work in reverse stocking stitch, decreasing 1 stitch at each end of 1st and every 6th row until 68 stitches remain. Continue without shaping until the reverse stocking stitch measures 25cm.

Shape top: decrease 1 stitch at each end of next and every 4th row until 62 stitches remain.

Decrease 1 stitch at each end of every 3rd row to 56 stitches, on every alternate row to 44 stitches and finally on every row until 32 stitches remain. Cast off.

Return to first set of stitches on stitch holder. With wrong side facing, rejoin yarn. Remembering which row of the fat cable you are on, continue without shaping until knitting measures 37cm (62cm from cast-on edge).

Shape top: decrease 1 stitch at each end of next and every alternate row until 16 stitches remain. Cast off.

With right side of work facing, return to last set of stitches on stitch holder. Rejoin yarn and complete to match first side. Cast off.

making piece I (cushion top, including the front gusset)

Cast on 70 stitches and work in pattern as follows:

Row 1: purl 3, work 64 stitches from Aran pattern, purl 3.

This sets the pattern. Continue in pattern without shaping until knitting measures 42cm. (Place a coloured thread at each end of the row after the first 10cm – this marks the 'fold line' for the front of the cushion as it is part of the gusset).

Shape cushion: decrease 1 stitch each end of next and every 4th row until 64 stitches remain.

Decrease 1 stitch at each end of every 3rd row to 58 stitches, on every alternate row until 46 stitches remain and finally every row until 32 stitches remain. Cast off.

making piece J (cushion base)

Work as given for the cushion top but continue until knitting measures 32cm before shaping the cushion.

making piece K (cushion gusset)

Cast on 15 stitches and work 137cm in moss stitch. Cast off.

making up the armchair cover

Weave in any yarn ends. Working on a large flat surface, pin the pieces out carefully. Gently press each piece with a steam iron taking care not to flatten the stitch patterns.

Join A (left outer side panel) to C (right back panel) and B (right outer side panel) to D (left back panel).

Join E (left inner side panel) to G (centre back panel) and F (right inner side panel) to G (centre back panel).

Join the inner panels E (left inner side panel) G (centre back panel) and F (right inner side panel) to the outer panels A, C, D, and B along the top edge of the chair.

Attach H (front panel), starting at the rib and work round the front of each arm. Finally sew in J (cushion base), pinning and easing as you go.

Sew on four pairs of tapes to the garter stitch back opening as shown.

making up the cushion

Attach K (gusset) to I (cushion top) first. Fold cushion along the line of coloured threads and attach K (gusset). Pin carefully, then stitch.

Attach J (cushion base) leaving an opening to insert the cushion pad, then sew opening to close.

beaded and sequined muffler

This simple but highly effective little neck scarf is made from an assortment of natural yarns – linen, hemp, cotton, silk, tweed and melange-effect yarns – joined in at random. No real formal plan or instructions are necessary for this scarf; the key is to select a group of yarns with colours and textures that personally inspire you, then add them in as you like. You may choose to select more vibrant colours to work with a favourite coat or jumper, or you may wish to recycle yarns from faithful old sweaters by back winding (see page 26). The finished muffler is strewn with wooden beads and iridescent sequins, sewn into position, to make a very individual accessory.

making the beaded and sequined muffler

materials

Assorted yarns from your remnants bag, all approximately medium or dk in weight. Use one, two or three strands of your chosen yarns plyed together to achieve the correct weight and tension (see page 25). The following yarns were used to make the muffler shown here:

Rowan *Linen Drape*
Rowan *DK Cotton*
Rowan *Chenille*
Rowan *Summer Tweed*

1 pair of 4mm (no. 8) knitting needles, or size appropriate for your chosen yarns
Approximately 100 iridescent sequins
Approximately 100 flat-cut wooden beads
Large sewing needle
Sewing thread

size

One size (approximately 102cm by 22cm)

tension

18 stitches and 22 rows to 10cm square over stocking stitch on 4mm (no. 8) needles. Always work a tension swatch and change needles accordingly if necessary.

tips

When working in stocking stitch, slipping the first stitch and knitting the last stitch of each row will give a neat finish that will stop the edges from rolling.

knitting the muffler

With 4mm (no. 8) needles and your chosen yarn, cast on 34 stitches.

Work in garter stitch – knit every row – joining in, breaking off and joining in different yarns at random until knitting measures 23cm. (When changing yarns in the middle of a row, drop the yarn no longer required to the wrong side of the work and join a small winding of the new yarn, twisting the ends of each together to avoid a hole. These ends can be stranded across at the wrong side of the work for a few stitches as you knit or can be sewn in whilst making up.)

Next row: decrease 4 stitches evenly across next row. *30 stitches.*

Change to stocking stitch, continuing to join in new yarns at random, until knitting measures 80cm.

Next row: increase 4 stitches evenly across next row. *34 stitches.*

Change to garter stitch, continuing to join in new yarns at random, until knitting measures 102cm.

Cast off.

making up the muffler

Weave in any yarn ends. Gently press with a steam iron, taking care not to flatten the stitch patterns.

Scatter the beads and sequins over the garter-stitch borders. Using cotton thread, sew the beads and sequins in place either individually or using long stitches across the wrong side of the muffler.

denim beanbag

A new twist on jeans with a jumper! Not to wear this time, though, but to sit on. Denim jeans have always been considered more desirable once faded, worn, patched and recycled. Just like its woven cousin, denim yarn shrinks and fades to a wonderful colour after washing. This beanbag uses both the jeans and the yarn in its construction; patched pieces of jeans are sewn together with ribbed knit pieces. The beanbag is made from six lozenge-shape pieces, three in denim knit and three in denim fabric, which are sewn into a large hexagon of fabric for the bottom opening and a smaller hexagon of denim knit for the top. The detailing is the most interesting to do; try to incorporate pockets, buttons and seams into your design to create a really relaxed and casual piece of fun furniture.

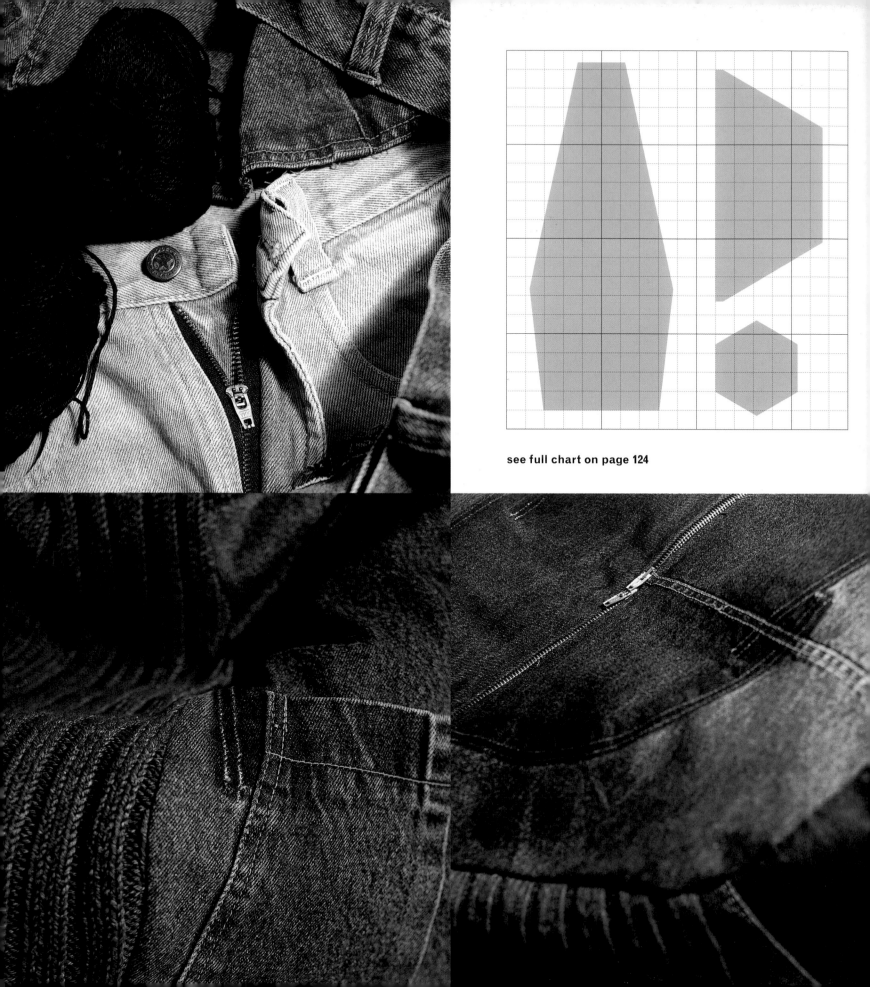

see full chart on page 124

making the denim beanbag

materials

Rowan *Denim*

  11 x 50g balls in blue

1 pair of 3.75mm (no. 9) knitting needles

1 pair of 4mm (no. 8) knitting needles

1 or 2 pairs of old jeans

Approximately 2m calico

Polystyrene beads

1 x 40cm or 2 x 20cm jean zipper or touch-

  and-close tape

size

one size (beanbag measures approximately 82cm high by 228cm circumference)

tension

20 stitches and 24 rows to 10cm square over stocking stitch on 4mm (no. 8) needles. Always work a tension swatch and change needles accordingly if necessary. Once you have knitted your swatch, wash and dry it following the instructions on the ball band. Measure the swatch again – you should now have a tension of 20 stitches and 30 rows to 10cm square. (The swatch should shrink approximately 20 per cent in length.) The instructions given allow for the shrinkage of the knitted panels only.

tips

Keep the patched denim simple, but incorporate pockets, buttons and seams for extra detail and practicality. If insufficient patch in another piece to size and cut all to shape. A 1cm seam allowance is included in the pattern pieces.

making the side panels (work 3 pieces)

With 4mm (no. 8) needles, cast on 60 stitches.

Row 1 (right side): * knit 3, purl 2, repeat from * to end. **Row 2:** * knit 2, purl 3, repeat from * to end.

These 2 rows form the rib. Work a further 6 rows. Increase 1 stitch at each end of next and every 9th row to 80 stitches, working additional stitches into knit 3, purl 2 rib. Work 3 rows in rib. Decrease 1 stitch at each end of next and every 6th row until 24 stitches remain. Cast off.

making the top panel

With 3.75mm (no. 9) needles, cast on 24 stitches. Work 2 rows in stocking stitch. Increase 1 stitch at each end of next and every 3rd row to 48 stitches. Work 2 rows in stocking stitch. Decrease 1 stitch at each end of next and every 3rd row until 24 stitches remain. Cast off. Weave in any yarn ends. Launder the knitted panels following the instructions on the ball band. Lay panels out flat and press into shape.

making the denim patches

Using the templates on page 124, draw out pattern pieces onto newspaper or brown paper. Cut 3 large lozenge panels and 2 half hexagon shapes. Use a strip from the jeans waistband to make a carry handle.

making up the beanbag

Sew short top sides of lozenge panels to knitted hexagon, alternating knitted and denim panels. Double stitch for extra strength. Sew two half hexagons together, turning seam allowance in at centre and inserting one large 40cm zipper or two 20cm zippers (with pullers towards the centre). Alternatively, use touch-and-close tape instead to fasten the beanbag.

making the calico inner

Using the same templates, cut 6 lozenge panels, 2 half hexagon shapes and 1 small hexagon shape. Sew short top sides of lozenge panels to small hexagon, with 1cm seams. Join all side seams of lozenge panels. Sew two half hexagon pieces to bottom edges of lozenge panels, leaving centre edges open but overlapping.

filling the beanbag

Insert the calico inner into the finished denim beanbag, attaching it to the inside at the top with a few secure stitches. Carefully fill the inner with polystyrene beads. Oversew the slit at the bottom of the inner to close. Zip up the denim outer. Squish into shape and relax.

hanging basket liner

String is strong cheap and readily available. Of course, it is wonderfully natural and biodegradable as well, which it makes it ideal around the garden. Here it is knitted up to create a simple, yet effective and functional, hanging basket liner for use inside or out. The liner, worked in basic stocking stitch on two needles, has an edge garter stitch slightly taller than the basket to allow for condensing once filled with earth. It is decorated with string pompoms. Plant with vibrant seasonal flowers, architectural grasses or striking euphorbia to make an ideal chic and economical gift for a keen gardener.

making the hanging basket liner

materials
2 x 80m balls thin parcel string
1 pair of 4mm (no. 8) knitting needles and
  1 pair of 4.5mm (no. 7) knitting needles
  or a 4.5mm (no. 7) circular needle
  40cm long
Large sewing needle
Cardboard
Scissors

size
One size (approximately 41cm in diameter)

tension
16 stitches and 21 rows to 10cm square over stocking stitch on 4.5mm (no. 7) needles.
Always work a tension swatch and change needles accordingly if necessary.

knitting the liner

With 4mm (no. 8) needles, cast on 128 stitches. Work 6 rows in garter stitch – knit every row.

Change to 4.5mm (no. 7) needles and work 12 rows in stocking stitch – knit 1 row, purl 1 row alternately.

Next row: (knit 6 stitches, knit 2 together) to end. *112 stitches.* Work 7 rows in stocking stitch. **Next row:** (knit 5 stitches, knit 2 together) to end. *96 stitches.* Work 3 rows in stocking stitch. **Next row:** (knit 4 stitches, knit 2 together) to end. *80 stitches.* Work 3 rows in stocking stitch. **Next row:** (knit 3 stitches, knit 2 together) to end. *64 stitches.* Work 3 rows in stocking stitch. **Next row:** (knit 2 stitches, knit 2 together) to end. *48 stitches.* Work 3 rows in stocking stitch. **Next row:** (knit 1 stitch, knit 2 together) to end. *32 stitches.* Work 3 rows in stocking stitch. **Next row:** knit 2 stitches together all across row. *16 stitches.* Work 3 rows in stocking stitch. **Next row:** knit 2 stitches together all across row. *8 stitches.* Purl 1 row. Thread string through these stitches, pull up tightly to gathe, leaving a long tail.

finishing the liner

Using the string threaded through final stitches, join side seam of liner.

making the pompom

Cut 2 cardboard circles approximately 7cm in diameter. Cut a hole in the centre of each circle. Wind the string into a ball small enough to pass through the centre hole. Holding the 2 circles together, wind the string round and around, keeping the strands close together. Work as many layers as possible before centre hole becomes too small for the string to pass through. Using sharp scissors, slip a blade between the layers of cardboard and cut around the circumference of the circle. Slip a length of yarn between the layers and around the centre of the pompom. Pull tight and knot the string, now cut away the card. Shake, fluff up and trim the pompon to shape. Sew in position at centre of liner. Make two or three of varying sizes, by using smaller cardboard circles and attach grouped together on a single string.

planting up

Mould the liner a little with your hands, pulling into position. Place in a wire basket or planter of your choice. Fill the container with potting compost and plant with your favourite blooms or seeds.

gardener's kneeler

A firm and functional cushion to kneel on in the garden when doing the weeding or tending to plants – an ideal gift for a gardener friend. The top is knitted in simple parcel string, which is matt in finish and gives strong stitch clarity. It is then embroidered with a simple running stitch in natural leather thonging for decorative detail. Authentic and natural colour hessian sacking is recycled to make a practical and durable backing: a coated sacking in a vibrant colour would make a durable alternative. The firm filling is provided by a piece of foam rubber cut to shape and tied in with natural cotton webbing tapes. Alternatively make a square cushion with a softer filling for use on a chair in the conservatory or potting shed.

making the gardener's kneeler

materials

3 x 80m balls medium parcel string

1 pair of 5.5mm (no. 5) knitting needles

Approximately 3m leather thonging

Blunt-ended needle

Approximately 50cm sacking, hessian
  or fabric of your choice for backing,
  70cm wide

Cotton tape for ties

Large sewing needle

Sewing thread

High-density foam rubber, cut to shape
  and mitred (available from most
  hardware stores)

size

One size (kneeler measures approximately 51cm by 28cm)

tension

13 stitches and 18 rows to 10cm square over stocking stitch on 5.5mm (no. 5) needles.

Always work a tension swatch and change needles accordingly if necessary.

knitting the top

With 5.5mm (no. 5) needles, cast on 65 stitches. Work in stocking stitch until knitting measures 28cm. Cast off.

finishing the top

Weave in any yarn ends. Gently press into shape using a steam iron. With right side facing and using the large sewing needle and leather thonging, embroider neat running stitches all around the edge of the top by working 4 stitches in and 4 rows in, placing an embroidery stitch in every alternate knit stitch. Finish with a knot on the inside.

making the backing

Cut the sacking, hessian or other backing fabric to the same size as the knitted top plus 2cm extra all around for the seam allowance. If using sacking, utilise the sewn edges of the original sack and you may wish to incorporate any authentic markings for extra detail. Turn 2cm to the wrong side around the edge of the backing, then with wrong sides together, sew the knitted top to the backing leaving one short side open with fine running stitches or blanket stitches. Sew lengths of cotton tape to either side of the opening, placing the ties approximately 8cm from the sides bottom. Insert foam rubber and tie cotton tape into bows to close opening.

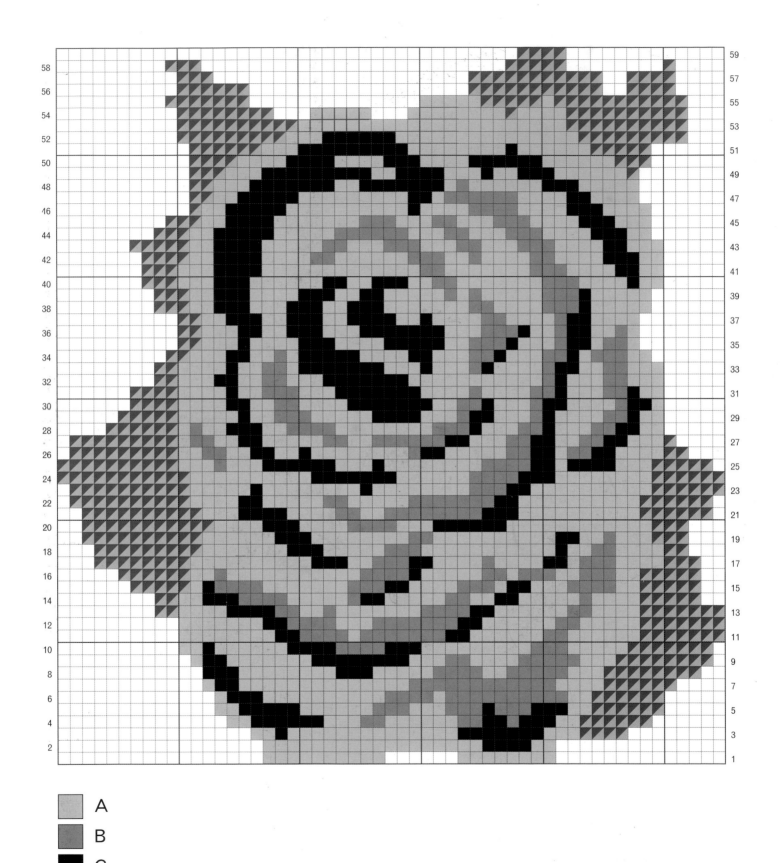

A

B

C

D

rose chintz cushion

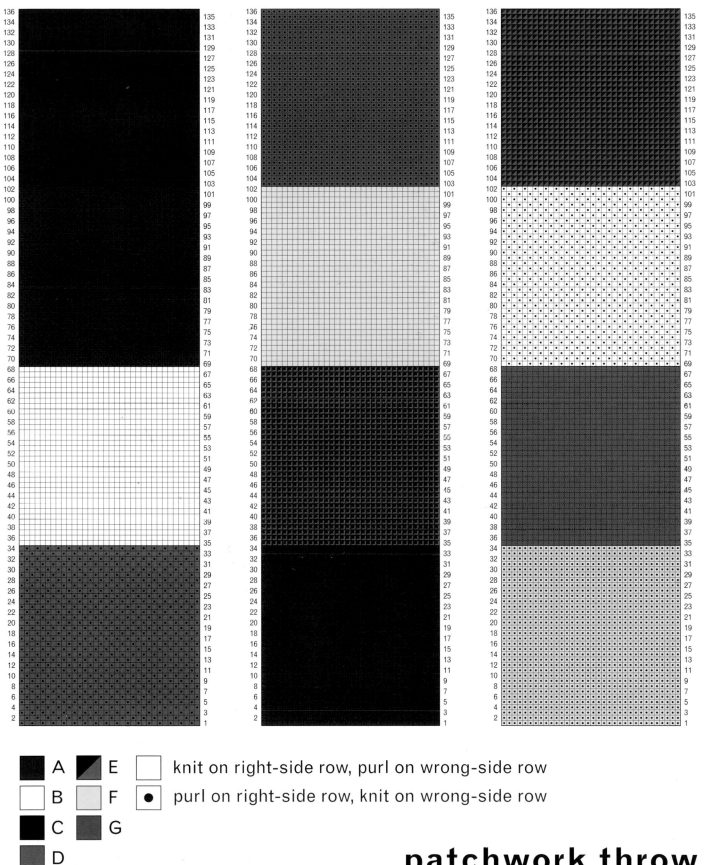

A		E	knit on right-side row, purl on wrong-side row
B		F	
C		G	• purl on right-side row, knit on wrong-side row
D			

patchwork throw

flower

 A

B

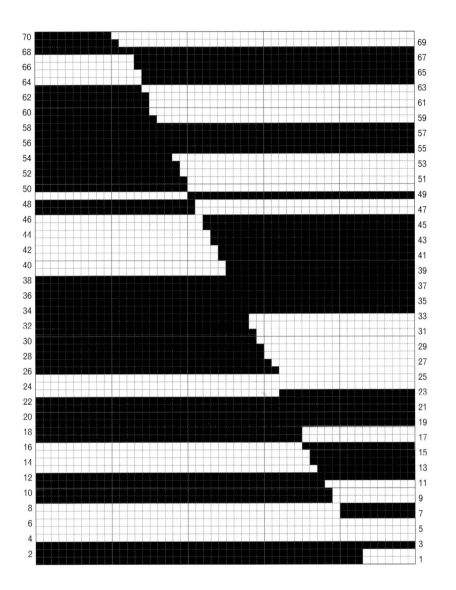

stripes

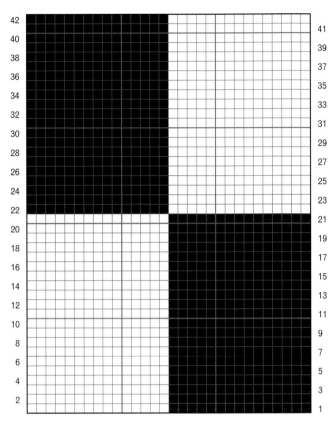

blocks

op-art wall hangings

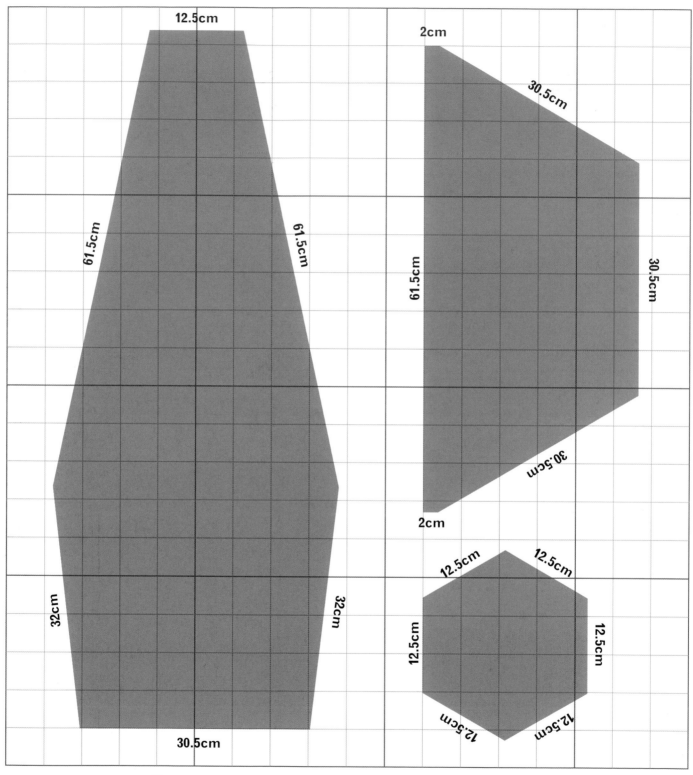

12.5cm

61.5cm

61.5cm

32cm

32cm

30.5cm

2cm

30.5cm

61.5cm

30.5cm

30.5cm

2cm

12.5cm

12.5cm

12.5cm

12.5cm

12.5cm

12.5cm

one square = 5cm

denim beanbag

substituting yarns

Although I have recommended a specific Rowan yarn for many of the projects in the book, you can substitute others. A description of each of the yarns used is given below.

If you decide to use an alternative yarn, any other make of yarn that is of the same weight and type should serve as well, but to avoid disappointing results, it is very important that you test the yarn first. Purchase a substitute yarn that is as close as possible to the original in thickness, weight and texture so that it will be compatible with the instructions. Buy only one ball to start with, so you can try out the effect. Calculate the number of balls you will need by meterage rather than by weight. The recommended knitting-needle size and knitting tension on the ball bands are extra guides to the yarn thickness.

other yarns

Metallic wire is available in craft stores or from wire merchants. The 24 gauge (0.5mm-thick) wire used for the Beaded Napkin Rings on pages 76–9 and the Moulded Wire Bowls on pages 88–91 was obtained from:
The Scientific Wire Company,
18 Raven Road, London E18 1HW.
tel: +44 (0) 20 8505 0002
www.wires.co.uk

Leather thonging is available in craft stores or from leather merchants/saddlery shops. The 2mm-thick round leather thonging used for the Recycled Plastic Shopper on pages 40–43 and the Gardener's Kneeler on pages 116–19 was obtained from:
J.T. Batchelor Ltd,
9–10 Culford Mews,
London N1 4DZ.
tel: +44 (0) 20 7254 2962

String comes in various thicknesses and is not always labelled with an exact amount, so you may need to experiment with a single ball to start with. The Hanging Basket Liner (pages 112–15) and the Gardener's Kneeler (pages 116–19) are made with parcel string, which comes either in 40m/44yd or 80m/93m balls, available from Muji, Woolworths and stationers.

Ribbon is available in a myriad colours and designs from habardashers and stationery stores. The ribbon used to make the Satin Boudoir Slippers on pages 80–3 was obtained from:
Offray Ribbbon
International customer service and orders:
tel: +1 (301) 714-4881
fax: +1 (301) 733-4981
www.offray.com
or
Berisfords Ribbons
P.O. Box 2, Thomas Street,
Congleton, Cheshire CW12 1EF
tel: +44 (0) 1260 274011
fax: +44 (0) 1260 274014
www.berisfords-ribbons.co.uk

yarn suppliers

To obtain Rowan yarns, look below to find a distributor or store in your area. For the most up-to-date list of stores selling Rowan yarns, contact their head office or visit their website.

Rowan, Green Lane Mill, Holmfirth,
West Yorkshire HD9 2DX.
tel: + 44 (0) 1484 681 881
fax: + 44 (0) 1484 687 920
www.knitrowan.com

selected Rowan stockists

AVON
Bath – Rowan at Stitch Shop,
15 The Podium, Northgate.
tel: +44 (0) 1225 481134
Bristol – Rowan at John Lewis,
Cribbs Causeway.
tel: +44 (0) 117 959 1100
Rowan at House of Fraser,
The Horsefair. tel: +44 (0) 117 944 5566
Staple Hill – Knitting Well,
105 High Street.
tel: +44 (0) 117 970 1740
BEDFORDSHIRE
Leighton Buzzard – Rowan at Needle & Thread, 2/3 Peacock Mews.
tel: +44 (0) 1525 376456
Luton – Kaytes Needlecrafts,
4 The Gallery, Arndale Centre.
tel: +44 (0) 1582 482517
BERKSHIRE
Reading – Rowan at John Lewis,
Broad Street. tel: +44 (0) 1189 575955
Windsor – W. J. Daniels & Co Ltd,
120–125 Peascod Street.
tel: +44 (0) 1753 862106
BUCKINGHAMSHIRE
Milton Keynes – Rowan at John Lewis,
Central Milton Keynes.
tel: +44 (0) 1908 679171

CAMBRIDGESHIRE

Cambridge – Rowan at Robert Sayle,
St Andrews Street. tel: +44 (0) 1223 361292

Peterborough – Rowan at John Lewis,
Queensgate Centre. tel: +44 (0) 1733 344644

CHESHIRE

Cheadle – Rowan at John Lewis,
Wilmslow Road. tel: +44 (0) 161 491 4914

CORNWALL

Penzance – Iriss, 66 Chapel Street.
tel: +44 (0) 1736 366568 www.iriss.co.uk

Truro – Rowan at Truro Fabrics,
105/106 Kenwyn Street.
tel: +44 (0) 1872 222130 ww.trurofabrics.com

Wadebridge – Rowan at Artycrafts,
41 Molesworth Street. tel: +44 (0) 1208 812274

COUNTY DURHAM

Darlington – Rowan at Binns,
7 High Row. tel: +44 (0) 1325 462606

CUMBRIA

Brampton – The Bobbin Box,
Unit 2, Old George Market Place.
tel: +44 (0) 1697 73611

Penrith – Rowan at Indigo,
1 St Andrews View. tel: +44 (0) 1768 899917
www.indigoknits.co.uk
Just Sew, Poet Walk. tel: +44 (0) 1768 866791

DEVON

Bideford – Wool and Needlecraft Shop,
49 Mill Street. tel: +44 (0) 1237 473015

Exeter – Inspirations, 7 Piazza Terracina,
Haven Road. tel: +44 (0) 1392 435115

Plymouth – Rowan at Dingles,
40–46 Royal Parade. tel: +44 (0) 1752 266611

Totnes – Sally Carr Designs, The Yarn Shop,
31 High Street. tel: +44 (0) 1803 863060

DORSET

Christchurch – Honora,
69 High Street. tel: +44 (0) 1202 486000
www.knittingyarns.co.uk

Dorchester – Goulds Ltd,
22 South Street. tel: +44 (0) 1305 217816

Sherborne – Hunters of Sherborne,
4 Tilton Court, Digby Road.
tel: +44 (0) 1935 817722

Swanage – The Wool & Craft Shop,
17 Station Road. tel: +44 (0) 1929 422814

Wimborne – Rowan at The Walnut Tree,
1 West Borough. tel: +44 (0) 1202 840722

ESSEX

Chelmsford – Franklins,
219 Moulsham Street. tel: +44 (0) 1245 346300

Colchester – Franklins,
13/15 St Botolphs Street.
tel: +44 (0) 1206 563955

Maldon – Peachey Ethknits,
6/7 Edwards Walk. tel: +44 (0) 1621 857102
www.ethknits.co.uk

Southend-on-Sea – Gades,
239 Churchill South, Victoria Circus.
tel: +44 (0) 1702 613789

GLOUCESTERSHIRE

Cheltenham – Rowan at Cavendish House,
The Promenade. tel: +44 (0) 1242 521300

Cirencester – Ashley's Wool Specialist,
62 Dyer Street. tel: +44 (0) 1285 653245

GREATER MANCHESTER

Didsbury – Rowan at Sew In of Didsbury,
741 Wilmslow Road. tel: +44 (0) 161 4455861
www.knitting-and-needlework.co.uk

Marple – Rowan at Sew In of Marple,
46 Market Street. tel: +44 (0) 161 427 2529
www.knitting-and-needlework.co.uk

HAMPSHIRE

Basingstoke – Pack Lane Wool Shop,
171 Pack Lane, Kempshott.
tel: +44 (0) 1256 323644

Lymington – Leigh's, 56 High Street.
tel: +44 (0) 1590 673254

New Milton – Smith Bradbeer & Co Ltd,
126–134 Station Road.
tel: +44 (0) 1425 613333

Southampton – Rowan at John Lewis,
West Quay Shopping Centre.
tel: +44 (0) 238 021 6400

Winchester – C & H Fabrics,
8 High Street. tel: +44 (0) 1962 843355

HERTFORDSHIRE

Boreham Wood – The Wool Shop,
29 Shenley Road. tel: +44 (0) 20 8905 2499

Hemel Hempstead – Needlecraft,
142 Cotteralls. tel: +44 (0) 1442 245383

St Albans – Alison's Wool Shop,
63 Hatfield Road. tel: +44 (0) 1727 833738

Watford – Rowan at John Lewis,
The Harlequin, High Street.
tel: +44 (0) 1923 244266

Welwyn Garden City – Rowan at John
Lewis. tel: +44 (0) 1707 323456

ISLE OF MAN

Peel – Fabric Centre, 2 Crown Street.
tel:+44 (0) 1624 844991

KENT

Broadstairs – The Wool Box,
66 High Street. tel: +44 (0) 1843 867673

Canterbury – Rowan at C & H Fabrics,
2 St George's Street. tel: +44 (0) 1227 459760

Greenhithe – Rowan at John Lewis,
Bluewater. tel: +44 (0) 1322 624123

Headcorn – Katie's Workbox, 15 High Street,
Nr Ashford. tel: +44 (0) 1622 891065

Maidstone – Rowan at C & H Fabrics,
68 Week Street. tel: +44 (0) 1622 762060

Tunbridge Wells – Rowan at C & H Fabrics,
113/115 Mount Pleasant.
tel: +44 (0) 1892 522618

LANCASHIRE

Accrington – Rowan at Sheila's Wool Shop,
284 Union Road, Oswaldtwistle.
tel: +44 (0) 1254 875525

Barnoldswick – Rowan at Whichcrafts?,
29 Church Street. tel: +44 (0) 1282 851003
www.whichcrafts.co.uk

Lytham – Rowan at Lytham Wools,
Unit 7, Market Hall, Market Square.
tel: +44 (0) 1253 732150
www.lythamwools.co.uk

Preston – Rowan at Bow Peep,
136 Liverpool Road, Longton.
tel: +44 (0) 1772 614508

LEICESTERSHIRE

Hinckley – Busy Fingers,
104 Castle Street. tel: +44 (0) 1455 631033

Oakham – The Wool Centre,
17 The Market Place. tel: +44 (0) 1572 771358

LINCOLNSHIRE

Lincoln – Binns,
226/231 High Street. tel: +44 (0) 1522 524333

LONDON

Central – Rowan at Liberty,
Regent Street, W1. tel: +44 (0) 20 7734 1234
Rowan at John Lewis,
Oxford Street, W1. tel: +44 (0) 20 7629 7711
Rowan at Peter Jones,
Sloane Square, SW1.
tel: +44 (0) 20 7730 3434

Barnes – Creations,
79 Church Road, SW13.
tel: +44 (0) 20 8563 2970

Brent Cross – Rowan at John Lewis,
Brent Cross Shopping Centre, NW4.
tel: +44 (0) 20 8202 6535

Chiswick – Creations,
29 Turnham Green Terrace, W4.
tel: +44 (0) 20 8747 9697

Finsbury Park – Lenarow,
169 Blackstock Road.
tel: +44 (0) 20 7359 1274
www.lenarow.co.uk

Penge – Rowan at Maple Textiles,
188/190 Maple Road.
tel: +44 (0) 20 8778 8049

West Ealing – Bunty's at Daniels,
96/122 Uxbridge Road, W13.
tel: +44 (0) 20 8567 8729
www.bunty-wool.co.uk

MERSEYSIDE

Liverpool – Rowan at John Lewis,
Basnett Street. tel: +44 (0) 151 709 7070

Prescot – Prescot Knitting Co Limited,
32 Eccleston Street.
tel: +44 (0) 151 426 5264

St Helens – The Knitting Centre,
9 Westfield Street. tel: +44 (0) 1744 23993

Wallasey – Ryder House,
44 Seaview Road. tel: +44 (0)151 691 1037

MIDDLESEX

Shepperton – Arts & Yarns, Squires
Garden Centre, Halliford Road.
tel: +44 (0) 1932 781141

NORFOLK

East Dereham – Central Norfolk Knitting
Machines, 4 Aldiss Court.
tel: +44 (0) 1362 694744

Norwich – Rowan at John Lewis,
All Saints Green. tel: +44 (0) 1603 660021

Sheringham – Creative Crafts,
47 Station Road. tel: +44 (0) 1263 823153.
www.creative-crafts.co.uk

NORTHAMPTONSHIRE

Holdenby – Patchwork Palace,
The Stable Yard, Holdenby Howe.
tel: +44 (0) 1604 771303
www.patchworkpalace.com

NOTTINGHAMSHIRE

Nottingham – Rowan at John Lewis,
Victoria Centre. tel: +44 (0) 115 9418282

OXFORDSHIRE

Burford – Burford Needlecraft Shop,
117 High Street. tel: +44 (0) 1993 822136
www.needlework.co.uk

Oxford – Rowan at Rowan,
102 Gloucester Green.
tel: +44 (0) 1865 793366

SOMERSET

Taunton – Hayes Wools,
150 East Reach. tel: +44 (0) 1823 284768

Yeovil – Enid's Wool & Craft Shop,
Church Street. tel: +44 (0) 1935 412421

STAFFORDSHIRE

Stafford – Amerton Farm,
Stowe by Chartley. tel: +44 (0) 1889 270294
www.amertonfarm.com

Wolstanton – K2 Tog,
111 High Street. tel: +44 (0) 1782 862332.

SUFFOLK

Bury St Edmunds – Rowan at Jaycraft,
78 St John's Street. tel: +44 (0) 1284 752982

SURREY

Banstead – Maxime Wool & Craft Shop,
155 High Street. tel: +44 (0) 1737 352798

Camberley – Army & Navy,
45–51 Park Street. tel: +44 (0) 1276 63333

Guildford – Pandora, 196 High Street.
tel: +44 (0) 1483 572558

Kingston-Upon-Thames – Rowan at John
Lewis, Wood Street. tel: +44 (0) 20 8547 3000

SUSSEX – EAST

Battle – Battle Wool Shop, 2 Mount Street.
tel: +44 (0) 1424 775073

Brighton – Rowan at C & H Fabrics,
179 Western Road. tel: +44 (0) 1273 321959

Eastbourne – Rowan at C & H Fabrics,
82/86 Terminus Road. tel: +44 (0) 1323 410503

East Hoathley – The Wool Loft,
Upstairs at Clara's, 9 High Street.
tel: +44 (0) 1825 840339

Forest Row – Village Crafts, The Square.
tel: +44 (0) 1342 823238
www.village-crafts.co.uk

Lewes – Rowan at Kangaroo,
70 High Street. tel: +44 (0) 1273 478554
www.kangaroo.uk.com

SUSSEX – WEST

Arundel – Rowan at David's Needle-Art,
37 Tarrant Street. tel: +44 (0) 1903 882761

Chichester – Rowan at C & H Fabrics,
33/34 North Street. tel: +44 (0) 1243 783300

Horsham – Rowan at The Fabric Shop,
62 Swan Walk. tel: +44 (0) 1403 217945

Shoreham by Sea – Rowan at Shoreham
Knitting, 19 East Street.
tel: +44 (0) 1273 461029
www.englishyarns.co.uk

Worthing – Rowan at The Fabric Shop,
55 Chapel Road. tel: +44 (0) 1903 207389

TEESIDE

Hartlepool – Rowan at Bobby Davison,
101 Park Road. tel: +44 (0) 1429 861300
www.woolsworldwide.com

TYNE AND WEAR

Newcastle-Upon-Tyne – Rowan at John
Lewis, Eldon Square. tel: +44 (0) 191 232 5000

WARWICKSHIRE

Warwick – Warwick Wools,
17 Market Place. tel: +44 (0) 1926 492853

WEST MIDLANDS

Birmingham – Rowan at Beatties,
16–28 Corporation Street.
tel: +44 (0) 121 644 4000

Coventry – Busy Fingers, 29 City Arcade.
tel: +44 (0) 2476 559644
Solihull – Stitches, 355 Warwick Road, Olton.
tel: +44 (0) 121 706 1048
Rowan at John Lewis, Touchwood.
tel: +44 (0) 121 704 1121
Wolverhampton – Rowan at Beatties,
71–78 Victoria Street. tel: +44 (0) 1902 422311

WILTSHIRE
Calne – Handi Wools, 3 Oxford Road.
tel: +44 (0) 1249 812081

WORCESTERSHIRE
Kidderminster – Woolwise,
10 Lower Mill Street. tel: +44 (0) 1562 820279

NORTH YORKSHIRE
Nr Skipton – Rowan at Embsay Crafts,
Embsay Mills, Embsay.
tel: +44 (0) 1756 700946
www.embsaycrafts.com
Whitby – Rowan at Bobbins,
Wesley Hall, Church Street.
tel: +44 (0) 1947 600585 www.bobbins.co.uk
York – Rowan at Craft Basics,
9 Gillygate. tel: +44 (0) 1904 652840

SOUTH YORKSHIRE
Barnsley – Knit Wits, 11 Church Street,
Royston. tel: +44 (0) 1226 725527
Sheffield – Rowan at John Lewis,
Barkers Pool. tel: +44 (0) 114 2768511

WEST YORKSHIRE
Castleford – Bromley & Vairy,
5 Vickers Street. tel: +44 (0) 1977 603069

Hebden Bridge – Rowan at Attica,
2 Commercial Street. tel: +44 (0) 1422 844327
www.attica-yarns.co.uk
Holmfirth – Rowan at Up Country,
78 Huddersfield Road.
tel: +44 (0) 1484 687803
www.upcountry.co.uk
Leeds – The Wool Shop, Whingate Junction,
Tong Road. tel: +44 (0) 113 263 8383

THE WIRRAL
Brimstage – Rowan at Voirrey Embroidery
Centre, Brimstage Hall.
tel: +44 (0) 151 342 3514

WALES
Aberystwyth – Clare's,
13 Great Darkgate Street.
tel: +44 (0) 1970 617786
Cardiff – Rowan at David Morgan Ltd,
26 The Hayes. tel: +44 (0) 29 2022 1011
Conway – Ar-y-Gweill, 8 Heol Yr Orsaf,
Llanrwst. tel: +44 (0) 1492 641149
Fishguard – Jane's of Fishguard,
14 High Street. tel: +44 (0) 1348 874443
Penarth – Rowan at David Morgan Ltd,
20 Windsor Road. tel: +44 (0) 29 2070 4193
Swansea – Rowan at Mrs Mac's,
2 Woodville Road, Mumbles.
tel: +44 (0) 1792 369820
Whitland – Rowan at Colourway,
Market Street. tel: +44 (0) 1994 241333
www.colourway.co.uk

SCOTLAND
Aberdeen – Rowan at John Lewis,
George Street. tel: +44 (0) 1224 625000.
Alford – Rowan at The Wool Shed,
Alford Heritage Centre, Mart Road.
tel: +44 (0) 1975 562906
Berwickshire – Rowan at Moondance
Wools, Springhill Farm, Coldingham,
Eyemouth. tel/fax: +44 (0) 18907 71541
Edinburgh – Rowan at John Lewis,
St James Centre. tel: +44 (0) 131 556 9121
Rowan at Jenners,
48 Princes Street. tel: +44 (0) 131 225 2442
Glasgow – Rowan at John Lewis,
Buchanan Galleries.
tel: +44 (0) 141 353 6677
Isle of Arran – Trareoch Craft Shop,
Balmichael Visitors Centre, Shiskine.
tel: +44 (0) 1770 860515
Kilmalcolm – Strathclyde Threads,
3 Drumpellier Place. tel: +44 (0) 1505 873841
Lanark – Strands,
8 Bloomgate. tel: +44 (0) 1555 665757
Linlithgow – Nifty Needles,
56 High Street. tel: +44 (0) 1506 670435
St Andrews – Rowan at Di Gilpin
@ The Wool Merchants, Burghers Closer,
141 South Street. tel: +44 (0) 1334 476193
www.handknitwear.com
Stirling – Rowan at McAree Bros Ltd,
55–59 King Street. tel: +44 (0) 1786 465646
www.mcadirect.com

author's acknowledgements
My sincerest thanks and appreciation to the many people who have contributed to the creation of this book. The truly inspiring and empathic team at Quadrille – Jane O'Shea, Lisa Pendreigh, Helen Lewis and Jim Smith. The talented and gorgeous Graham Atkins Hughes – everyone's 'favourite photographer' – and Raoul, of course. Sally Lee for her unswerving support, skills, tenacity and friendship. The exceptional Marilyn Wilson and Eva Yates for their pattern checking. Stephen Sheard at Coats for his invaluable contribution and all the team at Rowan yarns for their absolute support and assistance. Oh, and Freddy!

publisher's acknowledgements
Thanks to Elaine at The Glamour Chase Clothing Emporium, Kempton, Brighton, for help for the photography.